THE GREEN VELVET JOURNALS

7/12/04

For Janet,

Blessings on your journey. Be authentic and Remember to breathe! Know you are in my thoughts ♥

Kate Riley

The Green Velvet Journals

*A Mother and Daughter Journey
of healing, love, and trust.*

Vee Riley

Janet "Kate" Riley

Foreword written by

Lucia Capacchione, Ph.D.

In The Beam Publishing House / Idaho

Cover design & chapter epigraph illustration by Jessa Riley
www.jessacat.com

Authors' photographs by Jose Villa Photography
www.josevillaphotography.com

The Library of Congress has catalogued the trade paperback edition as follows:

Riley&Riley

The Green Velvet Journals/Vee Riley and Janet "Kate" Riley

ISBN 0-9749141-0-X

ATTENTION PROFESSIONAL ORGANIZATIONS: Quantity discounts are available on bulk purchases of this book for educational and gift purposes.

This book is dedicated to Sean Kevin Riley Mauk, son and grandson extraordinaire!

A wise young witness and teacher to us all.

Acknowledgments

To Lois Bristow, our visionary editor. Your expertise, patience, and love all contributed to a most endearing project. Bless you. To Lucia Capacchione, for your belief in us from the very beginning. Your loving guidance and expert advice on the publishing world, your time and energy in helping make this book happen, from our hearts to yours. To Janet Lucy for *always* being there for us with your wisdom and guiding spirit. To Ron Colone for your loving and supportive guidance. We think you're awesome! To Jeff Little for all of your expertise and guidance on the publishing world, even as it was given on the soccer field sidelines. To Jessa Riley, the cover design is fabulous. You're a genius! To Karen Riley and Nancy Martin for your energy with the emails during the final drafting. You're both angels. To Janice Miller for your love and continued encouragement, and for making it possible for the first print run. We can't thank you enough. Big hugs. To Laura Wilkening and Natalia Miller for buying the first and second copies of the book before it went to print.

Vee Riley and Janet "Kate" Riley

CONTENTS

FOREWORD

"What does a lump in the breast have to do with one's soul? Everything." These are the very words that co-author Vee Riley wrote in her green velvet journal during her spiritual journey through breast cancer.

The Green Velvet Journals is a true story, as it unfolded in the journals of a mother and daughter facing a devastating illness. It is the documented search of two courageous women determined to transform their deepest fears of illness and death into a spiritual experience based on love and trust, and a desire to deepen their relationship.

The Green Velvet Journals will inspire people of all ages whose lives are touched by cancer or any other life-threatening illness. It will appeal to journal keepers who know the value of this genre and are dealing with their own illness or that of a loved one. It will also support other mothers and daughters who are striving to strengthen their relationship with each other. This book is an invitation. It says: open to love, deepen your faith.

The authors are friends of mine who have become so much more. In sharing the development of this book project with me, they became great inspirations. I was able to move through the yearlong illness of my aunt and open to writing in new genres beyond the self-help field.

In facing cancer and her own mortality, Vee explored many choices and set out to find the lesson in the illness. At the same time, her daughter, Janet, learned to surrender to the mysteries of death and opened herself to new life. Their journey together, facing their worse fears, demonstrates how we can strengthen ourselves as individuals while finding depth in our closest relationships.

___Lucia Capacchione, Ph.D., A.T.R., R.E.A.T. Art therapist, teacher and best-selling author of 13 books, including *The Creative Journal: The Art of Finding Yourself, Recovery of Your Inner Child and The Power of Your Other Hand*

"There is a river that runs through our lives, an underground stream that carries our essential being. I have learned that once we enter into that stream, life is no longer lived in the ordinary sense. It becomes a journey, an adventure into unknown waters. Adversaries, conflict, and illness become teachers. Sleep becomes a time of magical exploration. Relationships transform."

__Hal Stone, Ph.D., *Embracing Heaven and Earth*

PROLOGUE

Vee

Finally, the shell cracked open. A fluffy baby chick burst forth. A bright new beginning.

I loved living on the farm, especially the Hildebrand Place nestled in the rolling hills of Missouri. My daily chores included feeding the chickens. In the morning, dressed in coveralls, I would walk through the screened-in porch, out the back door, and down to the chicken coup with my buckets of feed and water. In the evening, basket in hand, I would gather eggs for the next morning's breakfast with biscuits and molasses. Yum. It was there as a child that I learned how patient a red setting hen could be as she guarded her eggs. The year was 1937. I was 10 years old.

In the cycle of life we experience many deaths and rebirths, some small, some enormous. My story begins in late August of 1999 with the most monumental journey of death and rebirth so far experienced in this lifetime. My quest is to walk the path toward the complete truth of my spiritual being. In traversing this trail, both joy and suffering unite within the same breath. I encounter tunnels, canyons, mountains, bottlenecks, gangplanks, and ruts that hold the fears and doubts as I trudge along my way. Simultaneously, I listen to the quiet of the forest, marvel at the hummingbird, bask in the golden sunlight, and meditate on the undulating blue-green waves of the Pacific—each one soothing to my soul.

In my search, unforeseen junctions appear only to re-appear along the way again and again. Continuing in my trek, I persevere in my search. There are moments where I stumble over my own debris. Standing still, wishing to pull my feet from the darkened clay, I yearn for the light that will lead me to higher ground. Digging deep below the surface to find hidden clues, I struggle. Listening to the messages that fear and doubt create gives me the knowledge that something inside me needs to change. I want to embrace my shadow. The ego is a capsule that keeps me separate from the world around me. Only by becoming familiar with the deep dark corners of my psyche can wisdom and compassion emerge. This is my search.

It was late August. In two weeks I would be packing my bag for Idaho. What a nice gift I thought, as my mind replayed the phone conversation of a few days before.

"Mom, I'm giving you a special present for your seventy-second birthday. A trip to Payette Lakes in McCall." It was my daughter, Janet, full of excitement.

"What fun!" I replied, remembering the many summers we had spent there. "I hope Sean will be going, too," I exclaimed, picturing my grandson swimming in those magical waters.

"He's already packing his bag!"

As I was lying in bed on this fall morning, looking up at the skylight in the center of my pine-paneled ceiling, I watched the dark of night fade to the pale blue of morning. The redwood walls in my bedroom surrounded me with warmth and peace. I was grateful. Birds broke the silence as they announced the morning, filling the air with a joyous chatter just outside my window. I could visualize the furry squirrels climbing from branch to branch in the oaks.

I gave thanks for my four-poster made of cherry wood. I had purchased the bed at a local antique store. My intention had been to browse, but the bed in the corner of one room summoned me. A tiny lady named Theresa explained the bed's origin. It had come from Pennsylvania and had been made in the 1800s.

"Try it," she said while bending over to smooth the coverlet. As I spread my body across the mattress, I knew it was mine.

"One of my water colors has an antique frame that will fit in nicely here. Will you consider it for a partial payment?" I asked hopefully.

"Bring it in tomorrow for me to see," she said as we walked towards the front counter. The next day I placed the richly colored painting in the back seat of my classic red Volks and headed downtown.

"This will work," the shop owner said while reaching for her account pad. I was delighted when she ordered the "boys" to load my antique bed in the truck. The folks in Cambria are rich with generosity.

Again my attention turned to the skylight. I began fantasizing about the upcoming trip. Suddenly, the clock on the nightstand reminded me that it was time for my walk through the woods. I smelled the pines in anticipation. Throwing back my hand-stitched quilt, I rolled over and suddenly became aware of a lump in my right breast!

The words flew out of my mouth with no sense of direction. "What is this?"

Pure disbelief that this could be happening to me is all the emotion I can recall. Fear and panic were not in the process, only surprise.

Some call it denial. I call it stoic acceptance. My family background laid the foundation for this type of behavior. We had lived through the depression, braving some uncertain times without the display of fear. Our experience was one day at a time and this for me was a new day. With that thought, I placed my two feet on the floor.

Reaching for my heavy socks, I wondered, should I tell my family? This was my only fear. It seemed such an inopportune time, as though there could be a right time to find a lump in one's breast.

My daughter, Karen, and her family live in Boise and are excited about my birthday celebration, too. Gosh, I hate to ruin the party. But more important, my grandson Sean, whose father had died of leukemia only two months before, was in the midst of deep sorrow. He was only seven. How could I add to Janet and Sean's grief? Taking my terrycloth robe I walked slowly down the stairs to the kitchen, my mind scanning my options. I would face the challenge alone. I turned on the light, ground the coffee beans, and after flipping the switch on the Krups, sat down and ate a banana.

After breakfast I sat down near a window and gazed at the peaceful arrival of dawn. It was here that I began to take a good look at my life. For the most part, I was happy living on the central coast of California. Cambria Pines by the Sea is a magical town. My twenty-two year practice of massage therapy has been successful. Was there a message in this new discovery? A lesson to be learned? A calling that was being denied? I must not ignore a need for change. My mind is desperate for answers. With a deep sense of knowing, the path within would be my choice.

In the past, I have incorporated Reiki and energy work into full-body massage. Reiki, which means "universal life force", is an ancient system of healing originating in the mid 1800s. The practitioner uses a hands-on technique, following various energy patterns throughout the body. I had been feeling a strong pull to give up massage and move into full time energy work, but my ego got in my way. How could I tell my regular clients there would be no more full-body massage? I was stuck. All the while my mind was saying that I had to take care of these people who were depending on me.

The lump definitely caught my attention and created a change in my thinking. Still even at that, the transition moved slowly. I had always loved bodywork. That was my problem. Becoming too attached to one's clients is not good. They look up to you as a guru, which feeds the ego. I was courting fear and ego at the same time. The fear that my clients would be less interested created the fear of financial problems. I had made several changes in my life without experiencing fear. Why now?

My massage practice began before bodywork had been considered a part of healthy living. Upon completion at the Santa Barbara School of Massage, I found bodywork deeply rewarding. My heart led me to give up my desk job and pursue this exciting new field. Virgos need to be of service, and I was no exception. My private practice began in 1979 with no clients, yet I knew it would work, and it did.

After a few years, I moved to Cambria where I again faced a practice with no clients. Success soon arrived at my doorstep. Before long I had introduced a massage program to the local community college. My teaching experience combined with my love of bodywork soon gained approval.

Why then was it so hard for me to make a change now? My ego was having a ball. We were dancing to the tune of "Straight Vodka Every Night."

This served to block my spirituality, creativity, and self-knowledge. I thought I was happy, but my life was in a rut.

Finally, it was time to break free and advance toward my truth. "I am willing to change" became my constant affirmation.

Then one night I had a dream. A stone path was being formed, stone after stone. What appeared to be a nonphysical teacher handed me the first stone. The stones were heavy, but at the same time felt light. It was my journey into Self. I knew the way.

The trip to McCall was one to remember, filled with relaxation and meditation. I enjoyed seeing familiar sights, including the cabin we once owned. Janet rented a small fishing boat and made a giant effort to catch a trout. She wanted to teach Sean how to fish. Fortunately, the clerk in the hardware store baited the hook for her and told her where they had just planted some trout. She caught a small one, but was too soft hearted to eat it. She had promised me a bite, but I never saw it.

My surprise birthday party at Chuck's Steak House in Boise was one of the best dinners I have ever experienced. The restaurant is located on the Boise River and our table of nine family members overlooked a peaceful setting with ducks swimming calmly to and fro. I was happy.

Upon returning home, I held on to my secret and immediately began planning my art show to be held in early September. My friend, Lucia Capacchione, and I had already sent out the invitations. Since our in-home galleries were only a mile apart, it would be easy for our guests to visit both galleries in the same afternoon. The show was hard work, great fun, and a huge success.

Now it was time to face seeing the doctor. Dr. Wilson, a holistic physician, always greeted his patients in the waiting room. I was carrying the book, "Yoga of the Heart," by Alice Christensen. After examining me, his opinion was that some toxins had collected to form a lump in my breast.

"I would like for you to see Michelle Strasen, a surgeon. Also Amanda, an herbalist, who comes to my office twice a month. She can help with the diet."

I lay on the examining table for quite some time before breaking the silence. When I spoke, the words were as much for myself as for Dr. Wilson. "I can't see myself even walking through the door of a hospital."

"You will be able to, I'm sure," he said as he leaned his chair against the wall. "I had to."

I continued to lie there. He continued to be with me. I appreciated his time.

"I will be with you every step of the way, no matter what decision you make. I will be leaving for India in two days. I'll call you as soon as I return."

He kept his promise. Two weeks later the phone rang. Dr. Wilson spoke. "Just checking to see how you are doing."

"I have seen Amanda twice, but contacting the surgeon was not comfortable for me. It didn't feel right. I realize it is not following your advice, but if I go to a surgeon and have the lump cut out, I will never follow the design for my life," I explained to him.

The answer for me lies deep within myself. What is it that I need to know? I wondered.

"I am here to make suggestions, and if you don't follow through, I can be comfortable with that." An unusual doctor. Hanging up, I asked myself again, what is it that I need to know?

The following months were filled with getting to know my true self. Since I am a morning person, it was easy to roll out of bed and begin the day at 3:30 or 4:00 am. It was breakfast by candlelight while spiritual tapes played in the background. I was dedicated to the practice of mindfulness. The Buddhist meditation techniques helped me to face my challenge. Pema Chodron, a Buddhist nun, has taught me to relax with the uncertainty and to be with what is. This is the path I have chosen. My target is to become whole no matter what the outcome. A part of my sacred contract.

I opened my heart and mind in a compassionate way to my own suffering, as well as to the suffering of others. These quiet times generated profound bliss and joy. I experienced a deeply felt sense of who I was becoming. I was aligning my personality with my soul, opening my heart. I thought of the many times my heart had shut down. I was determined to uncover the wounds, both self-inflicted and created by others: parents, children, teachers, friends, and society in general. I was not attaching myself to the outcome, but rather gifting myself with all the treasures of knowledge I could gather, keeping myself on my path.

Four months had passed since the discovery of the lump and keeping the secret from my children became increasingly difficult. Janet and Sean were in the midst of processing intense grief. I would not tell Karen and Jessa, my other children, until it felt right to tell Janet.

With Christmas 1999 fast approaching, I thought I would wait until after the holidays. Our family enjoyed a delightful time together. On January 3rd, 2000, I knew the time had come.

Going about my morning activities, my heart ached and my stomach churned. I was nervous. Looking out the window from my dining room table, a scene so often cherished, I knew the challenge of today would be one of the most difficult of my seventy-two years. The squirrels and blue jays reminded me of freedom as they romped and played on the oaks in the back lot. Today, I longed with all my heart for that carefree feeling, but it seemed light years away. Today, I needed to face the phone call I had avoided for four months. The secret had been carefully harbored, pondered, and protected.

Now with heart pounding, I picked up the receiver and dropped it back into the cradle. How could I? I prayed for strength. Living with my reality was nothing compared to the anguish of informing my three children. How does a mother tell her children she might have a life threatening disease? A mother's role is to be there for her children. Now the role is being reversed. My self-assurance dissolves and leaves me unprepared. There are no books, no tapes, and no instructions. I sat alone with my frightened self.

Again, I prayed for strength, picked up the phone, and dialed Janet's number.

PROLOGUE

Janet

With Celine Dion blaring joyously in the background, I dance about the Douglas fir, taking each ornament carefully from its branch. As I place each one back into its packaging, I feel an aliveness I haven't felt for over a year. I dance and sing, every cell awakening to pure bliss. My heart no longer aches with lingering pain of grief and despair. I am living again. Reaching out to each ornament, I take in a deep breath and my heart sings. I am alive and bursting with joy, something I had doubted I would ever feel again.

The phone rings. I ponder briefly whether to pick it up or let the machine take it. I answer.

"Hi, Janet. Are you busy?"

It was my beloved mom. My best friend now. My mentor. The person I had called daily for the last six months since Sid had died.

"No, just taking down the tree. Actually, I'm glad to have survived the first Christmas and happy it's over. Maybe the next one will somehow be easier. They say it's the first one that's the most difficult."

"I know it's been hard. That's why I couldn't tell you of my situation sooner. It became important to call you, because I will not be able to attend Sean's birthday celebration at the end of the month."

My breathing slowed in silence. "Is everything all right?" I finally asked.

"I have something to say that is very difficult for me to talk about. It's taken me a long time to communicate these words."

Hearing the shakiness in my mom's voice, I realize the news is not good. I brace myself. Tears form.

"What's up, Mom?"

"Well, in August I discovered a lump in my right breast. At times the lump is sensitive, and I don't want to aggravate it by driving my car and using the stick shift. I would truly love to see Sean on his 8th birthday." I hear the sorrow in my mom's voice.

"In discussing this with my doctor, I have decided to go the more holistic way of treatment, rather than the traditional. There is no question but that I need to follow my intuition."

My survival mode kicks in. Defense flare. I take it as far as I can.

"Mom, I respect your waiting. I know how hard this must have been for you, especially knowing the intense grief I have felt over the past few months." Gripping the side of the kitchen counter, I realize I need to end this conversation. I can't continue. God, I need some distance. I need to hang up as fast as I can. I want it all to go away.

"So tell Sean I'm sorry. I'm going to call Karen and Jessa now."

"Okay." My mind races. My body frozen.

"I'll be talking to you soon, and I love you."

"I love you, too, Mom. Bye."

I was not prepared to hear my mother's words. I had awakened that morning feeling exuberant and alive, filled with a strong faith and a conviction to move on. In my journal that very morning, I had written:

I wash away the old and welcome the new. I am willing. I am open. I ask to receive guidance and to remain open to whatever comes. It is with joy in my heart that I move on. May I remember to love all and forgive all. I will begin by dancing at the dance studio. Go tear it up on the dance floor, Sweetie!

Hanging up the receiver, I sit and stare past the ornaments, beyond the tree as if it no longer exists. I am empty of all joy. I no longer yearn to dance. My breathing becomes forced. I am numb. Tears well and spill over.

"Why God? Why now, and why my mother?" I ask, silently and slowly withdrawing.

Rocked from my very own foundation, I feel as if the only thread that bonds my past, present and future is being severed. My mother cannot die. A new vista on life now whirled as an indistinct blur. Clouds of uncertainty blocked out my desire to dance and sing. A desire shattered in the moment, trailing in the shadows of my once cheerful spirit. The desire to celebrate life quickly dissolving. Tragedy was now inescapable and held me captive. I was paralyzed in the grip of fear.

My mother had waited four months to call. With the reality of it slowly settling in, I felt a mixture of emotions. Fear fills my chest and moves up into my throat. I choose to cut it off, forcing myself to breathe as I realize the courage it had taken for my mother to phone her children. The words I had spoken replayed in my mind.

"Mom, I respect your waiting. I know how hard this must have been for you, especially knowing the intense grief I have felt over the past few months." I flip back and forth, frantically between faith and fear.

The music is too much to bear. I turn down the stereo as if to mute my own existence. I am thrown again into despair. The Christmas tree's dying branches reflect my spirit. Lighting several candles, I pray in earnest for my mom. I know she is calling my sisters now. I pray for Karen and Jessa. As I sit immersed in a pool of confusion, I pray for strength.

During the call, I held together for my mom, my survivor once again coming to the rescue. But as I sit in prayer, something else happens, something unfamiliar. A force, a strength or power of some sort moves through me. I am calm and in the moment. I am not coming from a typical, reactive place. Am I

stumbling upon a newfound truth? I respect my
mom's decision in waiting to divulge the news and
her choice not to treat in the conventional manner.
Am I disengaging from it all? God, I want nothing
more at this point than to support her in whatever her
decisions are and will be.   I journal as a way to cope:

January 3, 2000

*I love you, Mom, with all my heart, all my mind, with all
my soul, and with my whole being. Thank you for
nurturing me and loving me, for being a vehicle for me to
enter the world, for allowing me to speak my Truth, and for
honoring that Truth. You have believed in me from the
first moment to this moment. I appreciate that. I am
forever grateful for your guidance, teaching me and loving
me all along. You are my truest friend.*

Two days pass. I am coping, but it is a
struggle. I teeter in and out of the reality of it all.
Reminders of my mom surround me. Her first
watercolor. It is small, but oh so beautiful. Next to it
is the old-fashioned, miniature wire-frame bed. Lying
in it is a stuffed "moose" with a red ribbon around his
neck. I study the hand-made quilt, each individual,

pink thread placed there by my mother's hands. It is a masterpiece. I find myself examining it closely, just as I examine the threads of my own life. Life is a tapestry of experiences. I feel as though I'm on the edge, preparing to weave the here and now into what has come before me.

I offer a prayer,
God, please help me to embrace this crisis with love and acceptance. I want to reach acceptance.

Without warning my mind leaps back to the conversation with my mom. It must have taken all the courage she could find to phone her three children. My mind races and then clouds with uncertainty. My God, is this truly happening? My mother's words now engulf me. I am lost as the news begins to slowly penetrate my being. I can barely sit with the reality of it. Taking in only bits and pieces of it all, I am compelled to walk through the old cemetery in Ballard. Maybe there I will find the relief my spirit desperately seeks. With God's help, I have transcended fear before. With God's help, I will transcend it again.

Arriving at Oak View Cemetery, I park in my usual place amidst the giant oaks. Suddenly, I find myself confronted with an unexpected anger that surges from my core and rages out of control. I am pissed, and I'm pissed at God! In this very moment, I will not compromise. I will not negotiate. Life sucks. My faith diminishes with every breath as I step out of the car onto the battlefield. This is it! I slam the car door and begin my walk. Moving forward, my body on fire, my mind racing, I walk with daring boldness and demand answers. I am ready and prepared to do battle with God.

"Come before me, God!" I cry to the Universe. "I dare You to stand before me here. I command You to show Yourself! You don't exist! You can't! If you do, stand before me NOW!" I yell out, defiant and unafraid.

I turn onto the long straight road on the outskirts of the cemetery. It is here where I have always asked God to join me in my walk. I plead for help. My rage dissipates. I stop along the Eucalyptus lined pathway and look up.

"Okay, what now? I surrender. Guide me to know what to do next. How to cope? How to stand up and continue on? Teach me, God, please, for there is a lesson in all of this, a gift, and I want to open it now."

Continuing through the old cemetery, I allow myself to feel the fears stirring so abruptly inside. With each slow, deliberate step, I picture my fears being released from my body and melting down into the earth. Repeating my mantra over and over I intone, "I release the old and lovingly welcome the new, for everything happening is part of the Divine plan, which I graciously accept. God, I want to feel it in my heart, not just in my head. Help me to do this."

I struggle as I consciously place each foot firmly on to the ground, allowing the fear to break itself free. Amazed, I feel relief, my fears trans-forming. Have I reached the doorstep of acceptance?

Turning to head back across the graveyard, I begin walking down the pathway. Overhead, massive Eucalyptus trees stand as sentinels. I feel God's presence with me and through me. We are one. I am comforted and at peace. I want to live in this moment forever, sustained by God's love and light. No pain, no sorrow, no fear. Only love. Pure unconditional love. I am filled with God's grace.

For the first time in my life, I find myself at peace, as if I have been waiting all along for this moment. Had I found a tiny entrance in a doorway to a path of acceptance? Had I finally stumbled upon the doorway? If so, could I walk through? Would that change how I approached life and death, bringing me closer to my own truth? An unmistakable, deep knowing filled me.

With each step, I watch the ground carefully and listen intently to the crispy sounds of fallen oak leaves crunching beneath my feet. I long to connect. I turn toward the back of the graveyard where centuries-old trees shelter ancient graves. Over and

over, I whisper, *I accept each challenge presented me.*
Dear God, please help and guide me along my way.

An inexplicable strength moves through me. I
welcome its powerful force.

A young couple with flowers wait for me to
pass. A man to my right waits to be alone in his
grief. Everyone waits afraid to act from the heart. We
are so afraid to act from our hearts in front of others,
to live in the moment without fear of judgment. I
recall the woman on Moonstone Beach in Cambria.
She was wearing a walkman and dancing all over the
sand, fast at first then slowly, spontaneously adding
martial arts, seemingly oblivious to those around her.
I couldn't help but notice her, to study her, to follow
her actions. Rhythmic and fully alive in the moment.
She reveled with an unrelenting determination
expressing herself freely and with pure abandon.
Was I free to do the same? Could I, as that woman,
dance in my joy? Could I also fall to my knees with
unrestrained emotion, surrendering to the depths of
my own pain? No, God, I don't want to separate joy

from pain anymore. I want to feel them when they are alive in me. For so long, I could not allow joy in.

I offer a prayer,

Thank You, God, for providing me with a glimpse of Your unwavering love. I accept this challenge. May it lead me closer to my own Truth through love and acceptance. I have no doubt You are with me; I will call on You to comfort me.

I leave the quiet trees and the stillness of the graveyard, reminding myself of the importance of transcending my fears. Fear depletes me.

I drive away at peace, knowing on a deeper level that I am exactly where I should be in my journey. I give thanks.

This is a new beginning. I stand on the doorstep of acceptance. Looking back in my journal entry for December 31, 1999, just five days ago, I was ready for the world:

I am willing. I am loving. I open my heart. I have all the courage I need to face and learn my lessons. I am ready for whatever comes.

~**1**~

THE JOURNEY BEGINS

January 3, 2000

A Note from Janet's Journal:

We are each on our own journey, and each is presented with intense and difficult life lessons. My lessons are different from my mother's. Each journey is unique, separate, and yet connected. I will ask her lovingly to take my hand as we navigate this long and winding road. I pray that God will be with us, fill our beings with love and light. For me, my hope is to find acceptance. I ask to be lifted, and when I fall to be carried.

For my mother ~ May God's love and light fill your entire being.

Bless you, Mom. Heal!

January 5, 2000

A Note from Janet's Journal:

What is the meaning and purpose of my life? What do I need to gain from all of this? I accept all things as integral to my spiritual evolution. I open to receive guidance. And so it is.

January 7, 2000

A Note from Janet's Journal:

Life is worth living. Thanks, Mom, for profound lessons on living. I love you.

January 17, 2000

A Note from Janet's Journal:

Ah, traveling the road less traveled enables one to remain true to oneself. So if it is Truth one seeks, the less-traveled road must be taken. Yet people stand in my way. People who want to stomp on me, to spit on me, and to declare their hatred for me. But I know, too, there are those who hold me, comfort me, nurture me, and love me. I open to them. If I am open, they will find me. Travel the road, Jannie.

February 16, 2000

A Note from Janet's Journal:

Don't give into your fears, Janet! Free your feminine power. Tap it! Nourish it! It has long been suppressed. Remember your immortal feminine strength. Let it flow. You are a woman with the heart of a warrior. Know that, Janet.

February 19, 2000

A Letter from Janet's Journal:

Dear God,

You know my every thought, my every fear. Grant me the courage to accept Your Divine plan for me, and the strength to continue.

I ask for healing of my mother's breast mass. I ask that You fill our very beings with Your love and Your light. Thank you.

February 21, 2000

A Note from Janet's Journal:

I sit in prayer and meditation, realizing that no one can take from me this moment with God. If I lose sight of this realization, I might crumble.

~2~

UNEXPECTED DARKNESS

February 23, 2000

Sean and I leave our home in Solvang. In a couple of hours, we will be arriving at my mom's home in Cambria. This is the first time we will see each other since her phone call with the news. I look forward to walking through the copper arbor just outside her small, redwood cottage. I smile, picturing her little, angelic face and white hair framed in the window. I imagine our loving embrace in the walkway before reaching her green front door.

A gentle rain falls upon us as we enter San Luis Obispo County. We stop along the way at our favorite health food store. I find myself becoming anxious as I walk towards the door. Grabbing a shopping cart, I grip the handle as though it were the only thing holding me up. Fear descends. I repeat my mantra, "It's going to be okay, Janet. It's going to be okay Janet. It's going to be okay, Janet."

Through the dairy section again, "It's going to be okay, Janet." Walking past the deli, I repeat it again. We leave. Wow, I am amazed and thankful. The immediate shift I made in this marketplace! Back in the car, calm and peace prevail.

As I venture along the highway, my whole being melts into the exquisite wonders of nature surrounding me. The hills are a lush green. Giant puffy clouds splatter above me creating a magnificent marbled sky. My van crests Highway 1. The Pacific greets me with turquoise tranquility.

Arriving at Grandma's-house-in-the-woods, I look for her in anticipation. She is not in her usual place, peering eagerly out the window for the sight of us. I miss her already. Opening the front door, I hear her blow dryer. Not wanting to scare her, I am quiet. I call in the direction of her stairs, "Hi, Mom!" The sounds of the blow dryer stop.

"I'll be right down," I hear her call.

I look up at her as she enters the kitchen. I am shocked and try desperately not to show it. She has changed. I barely know her. How is it, one day you recognize your mom and the next you don't? Why wouldn't I know that this could happen? I tell myself, it's not bad – it just is. This is difficult for me. I hug her and say, "You look so different."

"You haven't seen me since I called you about it," she says with a small smile.

"No." I'm barely holding on.

Walking over to a TV tray, she sits in the chair behind it. She is stoic, and yet there is a gentle calm about her. Glancing at the tray, I see the journal I made for her at Christmas. Beside it, a pen. The journal has three, purple, post-it tabs.

"Well, I'm filling up my journal," she says, lifting each section marked off by the post-it's. "I have affirmations, compassion, and gratitude sections."

I look at her. She looks so different. She has lost so much weight, especially in her face. My mind races to Sid. He, too, had lost so much weight before he died. Fear reverberates through me. Rage threatens my gut. Somehow, in the twirling, ferocious storm of my mind, I notice her skin. It is soft and healthy. She looks up at me. I can't speak, and instead, force a smile in her direction. I am overwhelmed by the desire to run, run--out of here as fast as I can. Out of this world completely. I can't bear another loss. Especially not my mom. I look at Sean on the couch. He is quiet, but taking it all in.

Moving towards him, I say, "Give me a hug, Honey. I have to go."

He stands and hugs me and then looks up at me to ask, "Mama, are you crying?"

"No, but I probably will when I get in the car."

I had planned to stay and visit for an hour or two before leaving Sean for the weekend. I had to leave.

Barely capable of forcing another smile, I leave, tooting my horn as I pull away, something I have always done. In the past, I always glanced into the woods, the thicket behind her house. At times, I witnessed a deer family grazing. This time I notice nothing outside of myself—no woods, no deer, no breathing in the smell of the pine studded forest. No. My mom is dying. My mind races in a flurry of turmoil. I cry. I cry so fucking hard I can barely drive.

The scene plays and replays in my mind. My mom, gentle in appearance, sits at the TV tray. She lifts the journal I made for her and points it in my direction. Her voice plays over and over in my confused state of mind, "I have Affirmations, Compassion, and Gratitude sections."

In desperation, I offer a prayer,

God, I speak to You now! Listen to me! I am hurting! Can't You see it! Why no warning? God, please take this hurt from me. Haven't I had enough? I can't face this!

Continuing on Highway 1, I visualize my mom watching her TV, only 15 minutes of news. She hears just enough to pray for someone and sends them compassion. She includes even the rapists and murderers. Suddenly, I see her in a moment of pure love and offering compassion for those in need. I see her clearly in my mind. She is beautiful, angelic, a living saint.

Surrendering, I head home, feeling faint and exhausted. I choose to be in the moment.

~ 3 ~

FACING THE CRISIS

February 24, 2000

Awakening early, I decide to abandon my plans for the workshop. I must return to Cambria. I will face my mom. I want her to know where I am coming from. I want desperately to know where she is coming from.

God, help me through this, please. I love her
so much. It is time. Life is definitely not about
power, control, or money. It is about love, and only
about love.

Telephoning a good friend who has known my
mom for many years, I tell her the news. She
understands. She says, "I'm not ready to deal with
losing my mom. I can't imagine my life without her."

I knew she meant well, but damn it, I'm not
ready either. Yet I have no choice! This crisis is upon
me. I can deal with it in one of two ways; I can face it,
or I can run from it. I will never again turn my back
and run. No. I will face it. I will leave for Cambria,
but first a walk in Ballard. I head down the long,
straight, familiar road.

I offer a prayer,

*God, walk with me, please. I realize once again, this road is
mine alone to walk, but I need Your help. I must do the
work, knowing You are with me, guiding me, and loving
me.*

Continuing on, I realize I must confront my mom's challenge and her mortality as well as my own. I plan to spend the night with her, plan to ask her straight out how she feels, to reach out to her and be there for her. I will not turn my back again and be held captive in my own prison yard.

I am grateful that I have some warning. For many, there is none. I will go to Cambria today with God at my side. I ask God for the courage and the strength to make this trip. I ask God for loving support and guidance. What will I need to share with my mom? What must I say? What must I ask? I ran from it just yesterday. My greatest fear now is the reality that my beloved mother could die. I will face this fear.

Driving north to Cambria, I reflect on my life. Even in the pain of my world today and even facing the reality of my mother's illness, I regret none of it. Not the pain, or the agony, for they lead me to Truth. Truth is my ultimate destiny. I will not stop. I will persevere.

I knock on the door. Sean answers with a big smile. I hug him. I hug my mom.

"Mom, I'm sorry I had to leave yesterday. You looked so different, and I couldn't handle it."

"It's okay. I was fine with it." Amazing, but she really does seem fine with it. How is this possible? Does she pick up on my feelings?

Later that night, the three of us sit down for dinner. We light a lavender/rosemary candle to float amongst rose petals in my mom's gold and crystal bowl. Joining hands, our eyes connect with each other, forming a bond. We individually express our gratitude. When my turn comes, tears rush forth.

"I am grateful for you, Mom."

I couldn't speak anymore, although I had tons I wanted to say. I wanted to plead with her not to move on. I wanted to strike a bargain with God. Anything. We smiled, despite my tears and raised our glasses in a toast. I found myself wanting to speak and silently asked God for the strength to do so. Words came from my heart.

"Mom, what's it like living with a foreign substance in your body not knowing if it's cancer?"

"Life is uncertain for each of us. I am living with my condition. We are never given the outcome. If we were, there would be no incentive to grow as an individual. This is my quest."

"I can't imagine what it would be like to face your own death. Aren't you afraid?"

"I am not afraid to die. Death is only a transition. Look at it this way. I will be graduating from earth school."

We smile with a deeper knowing of truth, and raise our glasses in another toast.

Sean sits quietly eating, taking it in. I was glad he was with us. He had wanted this, "a heart-to-heart talk" from his father, but Sid couldn't go there. It would have meant facing his mortality and that was something he couldn't do until the very end. Here Sean was witnessing "a heart-to-heart talk" between mother and daughter. I knew that hearing his grandmother speak would be healing for him.

~ 4 ~

THE DANCE BETWEEN FAITH AND DOUBT

February 28, 2000

A Note from Janet's Journal:

God, please help me.

Picking up the phone I call my friend, Christie. I hang up. Shit! I can't believe this! I don't want to hear it. Her mother died just last month from breast cancer. I wanted desperately to feel compassion for her, but my own fears won out. I pick up the receiver and dial.

"Hi Mom. I'm scared." Tears form quickly.

Lovingly, she assures me, "I'm confident in choosing the right way to go. All the studying I am doing, working more toward enlightenment. Wherever this takes me is where I'm supposed to be. I feel fine. This could go on for a long time."

I hang up, feeling better. I am also aware that her words do nothing to ease my fears. In desperation,

I offer a prayer,

Please help me dear God, please. I don't want to fight it anymore. I give in, trusting in You, the Divine. Carry me through. I need to mourn – yes, still and again!

Walking into my garden for a moment of reprieve, I feel desperately alone. What do I need? I must answer my own questions. The answers lie within me. I know it! My sojourn is revealing a truth.

In the midst of this tangled web, I am breaking free. I have lived for so long in a bubble of fear.

Sitting in my garden I explore my surroundings. I wallow in the beauty and the love that is here. Abundance is everywhere. Let it surround you, Janet, envelope you, saturate you. Let it hold you. Allow it to carry you through. Go buy yourself an armload of flowers. Place them everywhere in your home. Play in it. Frolic in it. Dance in it. I invite my soul to dance!

February 29, 2000

A Note from Janet's Journal:

My idea about sending my mom a journal feels good. I want to write my experience of my process while she is writing about hers. I desperately seek to know her thoughts.

Driving down the country road after dropping Sean at school, tears form easily as I think about my mom. It feels good, however, a release. I wonder how much pain and sorrow my heart can take. I must remember to care for my heart. I wish I could talk to my dad.

March 2, 2000

A Note from Janet's Journal:

After two months of dancing between faith and doubt, I find myself immersed in the dregs of an underground slue, swimming in a whirlpool filled with shock and reality. I know that I have yet to step through the door of acceptance.

For now, I offer a prayer,

God, how is it possible to find love and joy in life? How is it possible to have fun while mired in pain?
God, why can't I find acceptance in all of this? I don't want to be consumed by my pain any longer. Please, guide me. Please. I realize I have no control. God, I give in. I know no matter what I do, I cannot keep my mother alive forever. Please teach me to accept this. Teach me to be patient. Walk with me. I invite You to be with me at every moment of my life. Thank You. And so it is.

~ 5 ~

ANGELIC GUIDANCE

Returning home, I follow my intuition to swing into
my favorite local bookstore. I advance towards the
wall lined with the most beautiful assortment of
journals, all of varying sizes, all varying in color and
texture. My eyes fall upon a large, green, velvety

journal. I reach for it and am taken by its beauty. Gently caressing the cover with my fingers, I open it. It is the one.

Joining others in line to make my purchase, my thoughts trail off. Clutching the green velvet journal to my heart, I realize what it will be used for. I will write letters to my mom. Yes, I will bare myself on these pages during times I cannot speak my truth. Tears trickle down my cheeks as I turn to the person behind me.

"Will you please hold my place in line?"

"Yes," replies the somewhat bothered man standing behind me.

I run to the wall and grab another green velvet journal. Returning to the slow moving line, I thank him. He ignores me. It makes no difference. I stand clutching both of the journals close to my heart. I will write letters to my mom and letters to God in my green journal. Yes! I will send the other green journal to my mom. Maybe if I gift her this green velvet journal, she will write her story, and just maybe, she will live a little bit longer.

Returning home, I feel relieved when I hear her soft voice on my answering machine, "I am staying in the present moment. It feels right. Love you, Janet!"

Smiling, I take my mom's journal and with pen in hand, open the cover.

~ 6 ~

DEEPENING THE SPIRITUAL CONNECTION

The Green Velvet Journals

March 3, 2000

For My Beloved Mom,

    Another journal for you. I have one just like it and plan to begin using it right away. Having decided to fill it with memoirs, mostly of you and me,

I hope to include the painful as well as joyful moments in our lives, both past and present.

It is truly a gift to be able to experience each other's pains and joys at this time in our lives. Do what feels right for you in your journal — I know you will know.

May you experience pure bliss.

Love you, Janet

March 5, 2000

To My Beloved Daughter,

Thank you for my green, velvet journal. The design is so special because the patterns change with the reflected light, reminding me of the dark and light within my own life. I have chosen to keep it as a daily log, recording my progress on the road to enlighten-ment.

The journey into wellness began a few months ago, and since that time, I have embraced my assignment by following my intuition, and day by day have observed the opening of my heart. In this journal, I will record feelings and inspirations as I open to what is.

With Love, Mom

A Note from Vee's Journal, *Evening entry*:

In the beginning, I used lots of compresses of cabbage and green clay, as well as Castor oil packs. Acupressure and Reiki have helped tremendously. Today, the lump is still there, but the rest of my body is full of vitality. My early morning walks and meditation each day keep me in a state of ecstasy.

Thank you, Universe, for your gift of healing. As I listen to the wind chimes outside my back door, they remind me of movement, always changing. If we allow it, the melody can be beautiful, filled with peace and harmony.

March 5, 2000

A Letter from Janet's Journal:

Dear Mom,

Thank you for allowing me to walk with you. I was tempted just then to write: along your path of uncertainty. But it isn't "uncertain" at all. Some things are certain— we are never alone. Our spirits do not die.

Continue to teach me all that you are experiencing. You are wise—an elder and the Crone. You are also the most courageous person I have ever known. Your humility, your compassion for others, your love for all shines. You are a beacon of light. May this light continue to spread.

May you continue to find joy and to experience pure bliss along your path. May your soul continue to dance through the woods.

I love you with all my heart,

Janet

I offer a prayer,

Dear God, Thank You for this. It is truly a gift, a gift not only to be cherished forever, but a gift to learn by. I ask for a deeper understanding and in that, a deeper meaning for life itself. Thank You very much. And so it is. Divine healing in my life is now taking place.

March 7, 2000

A Letter from Janet's Journal:

Dear Mom,

I wonder how you are today. Are you worried, sad, angry, creative, full of joy? I don't think anyone can know how you feel when facing a lump in your breast, except for all of those who have faced it.

You said something the other day about the fact that the lump is still there. Though it is difficult, I appreciate your willingness to share with me some of your thoughts on how you are choosing to deal with it. I so admire your courage.

I love you with all my heart, always,

Janet

I offer a prayer,

Dear God, I ask you to fill my mom with your love and light and an abundance of strength and courage. Thank You so much. My life is so full of Joy.

March 8, 2000

A Note from Vee's Journal:

After losing twenty-five pounds with a strict diet of grains, nuts, greens, sprouts, fruits, and veggies, I feel the need for a change. My mind travels back to a scene at a local department store. While in the dressing room trying on a bra, I witnessed a horrifying reflection in the mirror. Looking closely into my face I ask, is it really me? The image staring back at me was that of a skeleton. Although it was painful to observe my shallow face, I was aware of a deep cleansing. I died to my old Self.

Becoming too paranoid about my diet, I decide to loosen up a bit. Today, it will be apple pie and whipped cream.

March 9, 2000

A Note from Janet's Journal:

Life is brief - be sure to Love

A Letter from Janet's Journal, *same day*:

Dear Mom,

After inviting you along on the Tahiti trip yesterday, I couldn't help but reflect on what you said. There were two things that stood out for me. One—it was difficult for you to plan that far ahead. Suddenly, I found myself in two schools of thought. It seemed okay hearing this, as you, over the last several years, have not wanted to plan too many things far in advance. But then my mind jumped to, My God, what if she dies before then? I can't even imagine my life without you being here. It makes me sad, and I want my tears to gush, but they won't. They refuse for now. Then you mentioned the money part of it. For me, money has nothing to do with it. If I had to pay for that trip for the rest of my life, I would. I love you so much. I wish I could cry. Tears lie cradled in my eyelids, refusing to flow.

I offer a sincere prayer,

Dear God, please hold my mom today and everyday. Thank You.

March 10, 2000

A Letter from Janet's Journal:

I love you, Mom, so much. I cherish every moment you are here.

Janet

March 13, 2000

A Note from Janet's Journal:

Today, I set my intentions:

- *Embracing the dying process and death itself*
- *Choosing to walk alongside my mom's experience and to learn everything I need along the way*
- *Transforming the fear into acceptance*
- *To find love*
- *To be guided toward my life purpose*

Tonight, I dance alone in my kitchen. I am fully in my body, expression flowing freely - my beauty, my love, my pain – all enmeshed in this sojourn of facing the loss of my beloved mom. A ceremonial dance – a prayer in motion.

March 15, 2000

A Note from Vee's Journal:

I am sending you love today, Janet and Sean. Thank you so much for the patio furniture. I love it. Yesterday, the sun was warm enough for me to sit outside.

This morning I was wide awake a little after 3:00 am. As I arose for my usual meditation, I glanced out my bathroom window. The stars twinkled at me through the pine trees and let me know that I was not alone. I wanted more. Grabbing my pink chenille robe, I walked out onto my upstairs deck. I opened to embrace the energy from the indigo sky. This has become one of my favorite rituals.

March 16, 2000

A Letter from Vee's Journal:

Dear Janet,

You called today to express grief over me. I wish you could be spared from suffering. Every mother wants her children to be well and happy, but life has taught me that this cannot always be. It is my desire to be there for you, and I will be there, both in life and in death. Accepting death brings true joy. We each have a path to follow. Sometimes we veer off course, but when we return and follow our inner guidance, we feel at home with ourselves and with God.

March 17, 2000

A Note from Vee's Journal:

Today, I saw four deer, "Sisters of the Forest," grazing alongside me as I sat on my favorite tree stump and meditated. They looked at me with no fear. Every once in awhile they would glance my way and size me up, and then with a quick flick of the tail, go on munching. I sit on the tree stump, taking in the ocean, the pines, and the aroma of newly cut grass.

March 18, 2000

A Letter from Janet's Journal:

Dear Mom,

I loved how you described your walk earlier in the day, how you sat on your favorite tree stump watching the four deer eat nearby, and, how you had a thought that perhaps I had never grieved your divorce from my father. As I was driving to see Louise for a much needed massage, I broke down and cried. I could feel it for the first time. Unresolved grief repressed for all these years. Thank you, for giving me permission. It felt good to acknowledge it, to finally own it, and let it go. During our initial conversation, I had thought perhaps it was your grief, and I was unwilling to accept it as my own. For thirty years, I had held on to this. Releasing this fragment of painful memory brought me one step closer to the whole of my life. I will continue to invest my Spirit in the present moment.

Something lies ahead. Could it be I am finally capable of taking the first step through the door of acceptance?

Thanks, Mom, for all that you have taught me. Your courage is profound. You are the most courageous person I have ever known. Your Faith, your trust, your love have all helped bring me to where I am today. I am forever grateful.

I ask God that you live the remainder of your life filled with joy. May God bless you with love and light and shower you with grace.

I love you with all my heart. May you always shine.

March 20, 2000

A Note from Janet's Journal:

My academic paper on "letting go" is due. I face the most difficult hurdle, the challenge of "letting go" of my mom. I ask for strength to cope.

I love you, Mom. I will always appreciate your kindness, your wisdom, your enduring patience, and your incredible love of life. I am so happy I chose you, and I am thankful for the opportunity to finally get to know you. Through knowing you, I have begun the process of getting to know myself. What a gift!

March 22, 2000

A Note from Vee's Journal:

I am the sum of my actions. Somehow, I feel that life has a new meaning. Again, my day of learning began at 3:00 a.m. Listening to Thich Nhat Hanh, a wise teacher from Viet Nam who practices mindfulness, has taught me an exercise of breathing in and breathing out. On the in-breath, I am to think of my eyes. On the out-breath, I am to smile to my eyes. Then, on the in-breath, I am a flower. On the out-breath, I am fresh. Learning to smile is so important. Smiling into my fear is a new way of looking into it deeply. Hello fear. Let's become friends. I no longer want to shove you away. Here, take my hand.

March 24, 2000

A Letter from Janet's Journal:

Dear Mom,

I feel sad that you won't be here for my birthday celebration. I am trying to accept the situation, yet tears well. I wish I could change every-thing.

Will you be here for my next birthday? The voice deep within my mind tells me otherwise. Why is it so hard to let go of those you love so much?

Tears begin to flow. My relief is only temporary.

Mom, I love you so much!

March 25, 2000

A Letter from Janet's Journal:

Dear Mom,

It is wonderful to hear you speak of your humility, your tranquility, and your joy. Talk about a gift of grace! You teach me much. You are beautiful.

Sean and I walked up to the base of Grass Mountain. The land there is sacred. The feeling, serene. I would like to take you there when you come down for Grandparents' Day, at school. We could have a little ceremony honoring life.

Sean and I went dancing tonight at the Grange. Such fun. I danced the whole night and we knew practically everybody there. As it was ending, they announced the next dance date, and you will be here that weekend. I hope we can go together. Will you be my dance partner?

I love you with all my heart,

Janet

"Dance is a freedom no one can take away."

__me

March 29, 2000

A Note from Vee's Journal:

Another 3:00 a.m. wakening. After breakfast I practice some exercises from John P. Milton's, Sky Above and Earth Below tapes. Milton's profound wisdom and shared insights help carry me through each day. In my anticipation to connect with nature, I pick up the keys to my Volks and drive to Moonstone Beach. Parking close to my favorite bench, I find it empty, as though just waiting for me.

Letting go of all distractions, I breathe in the freshness of the sea air and visualize the ocean waves washing over me with currents of energy. I open to this Universal life force as my heart and mind blend with the sky and sea.

March 29, 2000

A Letter from Janet's Journal:

Dear Mom,

It broke my heart when you explained you definitely wouldn't be here for my birthday celebration tomorrow. I placed the receiver back into the cradle and began to cry.

I offer a prayer,

I accept what is mine by Divine Order.

After repeating this several times, it dawned on me! *No, God, I can't accept this!* Again, *I accept what is mine by Divine Order.* Out loud I cry, *No, damn it! I can't accept the fact that my mom won't be coming. No, I'm also not ready to accept the reality of losing her!*

My mind counters, *you aren't losing her!*

A friend calls me from New York. In her soft voice she tells me that it has been twenty-one years since her mom died. She added, "But she is here with me all the time."

March 30, 2000

A Note from Vee's Journal:

Today is the birthday of my twin daughters, Karen and Janet. They, too, have a multitude of feelings they struggle to resolve. Each at her own pace, either in this lifetime or another. I had planned to drive to Solvang to be with Janet for her party, but the idea of driving overwhelmed me. When the plans were made, I was feeling great. However, last night the lump was bothersome. Getting in touch with my true feelings, I honor my body and change my plans. I feel as though I would be pushing myself. My spirit urges me on; my body says, "Take good care of me."

The sun is coming up, a new day dawning. A miracle every morning. The freshness reminds me that life is made up of the dark and the light. For me, the last twenty-two years have been light-filled. Now I must delve into my shadow side. So much pain and suffering in the world. As I tap into my own dark stuff, my heart opens to others. I wish them free of suffering. I, too, seek freedom from suffering. Buddha teaches compassion for others and compassion for ourselves.

Having decided not to go to Janet's today, I build a fire. Fire brings me warmth, peace, and happiness.

March 31, 2000, *Morning entry*

A Letter from Janet's Journal:

Dear Mom,

I meant to journal a letter to you yesterday on my birthday, but was upset you couldn't make the drive. When I brought it up with Karen and Jessa, I found myself distanced. I also realized yesterday, as dear as they both are to me, I am unable to go into the depths of sharing my own grief with them. They are where they are with it all, and I must accept that. Opening up at this time doesn't feel safe for me.

I give thanks to you for being my mom. Today, I realize how difficult it was for you. I can hear you rephrasing my comment and changing the word "difficult" to "challenging".

I am doing my very best at all of this. I love you, Mom. You are teaching me that only love matters. Thank you.

I love you,

Janet

A Note from Janet's Journal, *Evening entry*:

Happy Birthday Grandpa Denison! You would have turned 100 today! I love you, wherever you are. My mom gave me a most beautiful gift for my birthday. It arrived today, a day late, but just at the right moment! She put so much love into it, and now I will take part in it. I will honor her gift and myself, and make it a ritual.

My mom has so thoughtfully combined an assortment of things. Everything is wrapped in pink. Taking my gifts into the bathroom, I begin to fill the tub with Lavender bath foam and place the candles around the room. What shall I place on the altar at the foot of the tub? I smile at the small bottle of Sparkling Bubbles. Opening the soft pink chenille bath towel, I hold it close. Draping my new plush terrycloth robe over door hook, I turn and breathe in the aroma of Lavender. Delighted and soothed, I step into the tub and sink into the warm water. Bliss, the CD she gave me, floats through the space. I am in heaven.

April 1, 2000

A Note from Vee's Journal:

Attended the Mad Hatter's Ball with my friend, Lucia. I wore my old-fashioned tapestry chapeau adorned with roses. It was a fundraiser to purchase the East West Ranch on the bluff of Cambria. I donated a portrait of the late Warren

Leopold for the silent auction. Warren was an architect and had become a Cambrian icon. It sold. Maybe, I own one square inch of the land.

April 2, 2000

A Note from Vee's Journal:

After lunch today, I arrived at Moonstone Beach. The wildflowers that bloom every spring on the bluff scream out with color. An array of yellows and purples dust the fields that cover East West Ranch. As I walk along the boardwalk, I am reminded of a dream Karen once told me. She described how my mother had appeared one night in her bedroom and had said to her, "Tell your mother to walk among the wildflowers."

As I walk along, I think of my mother and her healing touches.

~ 7 ~

GOING DEEPER

April 3, 2000

A Note from Vee's Journal:

Today, I will search deep within myself to find hidden treasures. At breakfast, I studied the picture of me as a child. I wore the crepe-paper dress my mother hand stitched for me, and a matching bow in my hair. My Shirley Temple patent-leather shoes perched on the pedals of my decorated tricycle. I felt extremely close to that little girl and her desire to feel pretty. Love from my mother and a neighbor woman as they prepared me for the contest left my heart feeling all warm inside. The small town of Tindall, Missouri, celebrated with a "Corn Show" each year. It was designed mostly to see which farmer had grown the tallest corn stalk.

Throughout the day, there were pie-eating contests, sack races, the performance of a magician, etc. My mother entered me in the five-year-old parade. I won first prize. The judge handed me a fifty-cent piece. Each child had received a candy bar for entering. Loving candy as I did, I traded my fifty cent piece for another girl's candy bar. Fifty cents would have bought a grocery bag full of candy in those days. Oh well, I was happy. What a big-time spender I was.

I was about that age when my brother, Dwight, was born. His arrival was difficult for me. Dwight's presence changed everything. My mother no longer spent as much time reading to me. She held him on her lap instead of me! The things we have to survive as children, so sensitive. Also, since mother had given birth at home, she had to rest in bed for several days, or so they thought at that time. The woman who came to help with the household duties didn't speak English very well. I couldn't understand her, but it wouldn't be right for me to tell her so. I remember going to my mother as she lay in bed and saying, "She asked me to do something, but I don't know what it is."

Another glimpse of the picture reveals to me that I was a very sweet child. In school I resented being sweet. For good reason. One day I was walking home from school on a country road with my friend, Talma. She said she had heard our teacher say to her mother, "Velma really can't sing, but she is so sweet, I hate to tell her." That cut to the quick. After that, I didn't want to be sweet anymore. It meant that people couldn't tell you the truth. I was only in the first grade, but the truth had come out. I couldn't sing. Why didn't the warrior spirit rise up in me then? Well, at the age of 72, I am releasing it. Can you imagine being married to a clergyman, going to church every Sunday, and just moving your lips to the songs?

Isn't it sad that someone who didn't mean any harm can do so much damage to a child? I was only six at the time. This became a false belief I unconsciously clung to over my lifetime. My teacher was a good teacher, and I was fond of her. Perhaps that is why it hurt so much.

April 4, 2000
A Letter from Janet's Journal:
Dear Mom,

Mom, I'm angry. I feel betrayed by you. I feel betrayed by God. How can you expect me to accept what is happening, to lovingly walk with you down your path? My pain and sorrow run deep and will be there, no matter how accepting I am.

Somehow I can't go to that place of being angry with you. Somehow it is much easier to be angry with God. What is my lesson here? To reach into my anger, grab hold of it, and lay it out for all to see? My world has been shaken by your news!

Okay, so I'm angry. I'm angry with God, and anybody who has ever been in my life. I don't know what I'm saying. I choose to go walk in Ballard. I will take my walk with God down the long road there.

I arrive, and notice a funeral going on. This makes me angrier. How could anyone have died and planned the service now? I need to walk with God. Then I realize, I can walk anywhere with God. In fact, God is always with me. God is in me. I'm so confused.

April 7, 2000

A Note from Janet's Journal:

I am Divinely guided along my journey into wholeness and acceptance.

April 8, 2000

A Note from Vee's Journal:

Jessa, my daughter, arrived early in the afternoon. We went to Farmer's Market together. It was nice having someone carry my bags for me. We cooked hamburgers on the patio and after dinner watched a movie. I so enjoy her presence and miss her when she leaves.

April 12, 2000

A Letter from Janet's Journal:

Dear Mom,

Well, any minute you will be pulling into my driveway. It's kind of funny, because as I began this letter, I could smell your essential oils — as though you had just walked in. You arrive and look fabulous! It is truly amazing. Your hard work and discipline have paid off!

What a wonderful time we have together! Good laughs about my secret walk out onto the baseball diamond – hot flash and all! I will never forget telling you as you rolled on the floor in hysteria, Sean leaning over you, whispering, "Be careful Grandma, not to wet your pants!" We laugh even harder.

I am so grateful for each and every day we are alive. Thank You, God. I love you, Mom

April 13, 2000

A Note from Janet's Journal:

Okay, so I have multiple personalities! It's okay. I think it's expected, this bouncing back and forth. Ah, the extremes of being human, a way of learning about ourselves.

I come to my senses after a week, maybe two, of being angry with God. I've been so angry, I couldn't commune with God. I can't write a thing, because I am so angry. Now my anger is dissolved.

April 17, 2000

A Note from Vee's Journal:

My Rumi card for today reads, "Love is the Universal truth that conquers all". As I sit here in the early morning with the raindrops pattering on the rooftop, my thoughts turn to my simple life and to how much I love it. Yes, I find it a challenge to pay the bills, but what would my life be like if I had to worry about Wall Street and my money? Give me the simple life! With this space I have time to walk, meditate, nourish myself and my soul, and help others. I depend on synchronicity and the abundance of the Universe. I live well.

The unfolding of the heart is a life-long process. Sometimes, I think I'm just beginning.

April 19, 2000

A Note from Vee's Journal:

Walk lightly – stronger than ever before – will not lose perspective – confronted with own death possibilities – revamp what is being done at the time.

April 23, 2000

A Note from Vee's Journal:

Today, I feel very relaxed. My friend, Nan, gave me a Reiki treatment. Then I walked on the beach where I inhaled the fresh air, soaked up the sun, and enjoyed the pounding surf. I no longer feel the need to protect myself so much. The lumps are still here, but it feels as though I have cured whatever else was going on. It is like I planted the seed, tilled the soil, and am now reaping the harvest. My heart is filled with gratitude.

Easter Sunday 2000

A Note from Vee's Journal:

A beautiful morning, the sun is coming up through the east window. I had apple strudel and banana instead of my usual oatmeal for breakfast. I am feeling good, and the last few days I have been getting up a little later – around six-thirty. I don't need my learning session as much now. They have been so beneficial these last few months.

For everything, there is a time. Much healing has transpired with tapes, books, and quiet moments. Buddha's teachings have much to offer as I go through the dark side. Unity Village in my home state of Missouri has been supportive, praying with me on the phone as well as mailing positive thoughts that arrive just at the right moment, validating Jung's concept of synchronicity. We need interconnection with people, even those we never see! You never know when a breakthrough might happen.

April 26, 2000

A Note from Vee's Journal:

I went to San Luis Obispo today to buy a new pair of badly needed walking shoes. Found a pair just like my old ones. As I was walking by the Gap, the thought occurred to me that they might have stretchy jeans. They didn't have what I wanted so what did I do? I bought myself a pair of overalls! So exciting! I love overalls! They remind me of my days on the farm.

A deeper excitement resonated within me. For several months, I was unsure of my condition. It didn't make sense to buy new clothes if I faced my dying soon. It feels so good not to think that way anymore. Even though the lumps are still with me, I am less concerned about them. It feels okay not to worry. Buying new overalls and walking shoes was a significant and positive step. A celebration!

May 3, 2000

A Note from Vee's Journal:

Again today, I listened to a rainbow meditation by John P. Milton. Visualizing all the colors flowing through and around my body brought peace. Reaching upward and out to all beings and flowing back to my center brought harmony. Balancing the chakras, I felt aligned.

May 9, 2000

A Note from Vee's Journal:

Today is a day of reflection. The death of my son-in-law, Sid, brought memories of my devotion to Janet and Sean. It was an uneasy time in our lives. I felt my presence with them was meaningful and important. At the same time, my duty-bound nature created a hardship for me. I wanted to be there for my clients as well. Many commuting miles from Cambria to Solvang could have been alleviated had I chosen my priorities with clarity. Did I create additional duties for myself in order to avoid my own dilemma? It is quite possible. Since that time, I have sorted out what to shed and what to keep. Constant renewing of the spirit brings about a knowing in the time of crisis. Taking a few moments to go within can save hours of uncalled-for actions. A lesson well learned.

Now I must gather wood to build a fire in my cozy fireplace.

May 10, 2000

A Note from Vee's Journal:

May my life flow with grace and ease. May it be filled with love and light. May I experience pure bliss and joy. Remember to breath. Remember to nurture myself, to love myself, especially my body, the wonderful temple that houses my spirit. Treat it well.

May 11, 2000

A Note from Vee's Journal:

Pasted on the inside cover of my Green Velvet Journal from Janet is a card that reads: Simplify, Simplify. The truth is, I have simplified my life so much I'm hardly working. My favorite thing to do is work with people and their problems. This I do by a process called Focusing. This means getting to the feeling rather than the thinking process. Stored emotions linger on if not released. Gut feelings are sometimes the last to receive attention.

Focusing, combined with Reiki and Energy Balancing takes time to promote. Patience will win as each day sheds new light upon my path. Virgos are known for their diligence, and my mission is clear.

May 14, 2000, *Mother's Day in Cambria*
A Note from Janet's Journal:

So much to be grateful for. I am alive. I have an incredibly beautiful son at that memorable age of breaking away a bit and realizing his own potential. He could not wait until this morning to have Grandma bring me coffee in bed. What a treat this is! His father used to bring me coffee in bed.

We all gather on Grammy's bed. All of us in our jammies, I marvel at what a special time this is. Sean races to get more gifts from downstairs. Suddenly, Grammy asks, her voice concerned, "Where are your gifts?"

"Sean already gave me mine."

"Oh."

In this moment I realize another gift from God. Yes, my mom. I am grateful that she is here this Mother's Day. Two months ago, I actually believed she wouldn't be here today. But she is here—fully alive! A brush with death changes the lives of those close to you. I watch her and am reminded of her humility. She is so full of love and compassion. I am learning from her, but it is often difficult. Today, I am grateful.

We walk the beach to the tide pools and find half-buried treasures along the way. Sitting up on a large overhanging rock, I meditate and feel connected—one with the Universe. I am in the moment. This is life! Opening my eyes, I scan the beach to find Sean running towards my mom. She looks like she might be stuck climbing up a rock. He scoots past her and jumps down beyond her. Smiling, I give thanks for the moment and climb down.

Later, on my mom's deck, the squirrels break the silence. I still feel connected. I have no idea what my future holds for me, but I trust that things will be okay. I fare much better living in the moment and not jumping ahead. This has been difficult to learn.

At the close of the weekend, it became very clear to me...my mother will always be with me. I wonder how long this clarity will be with me.

May 15, 2000

I offer a prayer,

Thank You, God, for my mother. What more could I have wanted than to have shared Mother's Day with her one more time. May there be many more.

May 16, 2000

A Note from Vee's Journal:

Janet and Sean were here for Mother's Day. They spent two nights and didn't want to go home. Many shells were found at the tide pools, both at Moonstone and Lampton Park. I believe Sean is planning to make a shell mirror for his teacher. He likes her a lot.

We had lunch at Robin's. Janet was missing Sid and talked through tears. Sean helped clear the tables so the gals who work there awarded him with a piece of strawberry pie. I ate most of it. Sean would make a good busboy, although he would be talking to people all the time!

Janet brought me a beautiful bouquet of flowers, plus a Buddha prayer stone and two stones with "Blessings" and "Imagine," inscribed on them. Karen sent a Clinique make-up package, plus a small book titled, "Don't Sweat the Small Stuff." Jessa gave me some of her colored pencils, as I mentioned it would be fun to experiment with them. She is so talented in her approach.

All in all, I feel blessed to have three beautiful children who care. Naturally, there were times when my motherhood overwhelmed me, and I fell short of what I wanted to be. But there is no way I can change that now. I will just be aware of the present, as I have never stopped being a mother.

May 19, 2000

A Note from Janet's Journal:

I honor myself today in that I am making and taking grand strides on my journey. Embrace it, Honey. Look forward to a new day.

May 20, 2000

A Letter from Vee's Journal:

Dear Journal,

Why doesn't this lump dissolve? It seems to stay the same size. Even though I am so much better, the lump seems as though it will never go away. It takes patience, which I have had all along. Pema Chodron says, "Just be with what is." So my first duty is to own it.

Right now, sitting on my patio and listening to the birds sing, I am grateful for life.

June 3, 2000

A Note from Janet's Journal:

I feel so alone these days, as though I've been abandoned by God and my spirit guides. I know in my heart that this is not the case and realize how easy it is for my mind to travel so far from the truth. Am I being forced to deal with things I have always avoided? I feel powerless. I'm so tired of it.

Don't resist going with the flow. Relax. Breathe and go with the flow!

June 10, 2000

A Note from Janet's Journal:

In seeking guidance, I ask my spirit guides to be with me, to guide me, and to surround me with their love—God's love. I feel as though I have been derailed again. I wish to stay on track—God's track. I wish to do God's work. I want so badly to be a vessel for God's love. What has happened to this thing called trust?

I offer my prayer,

God, please advise. I consciously choose to step out into the world and continue my journey doing Your work. No more glass walls and isolation. There is only love, plenty of time, a vast openness in which to explore heaven on earth. I begin with an openness and willingness, knowing I will be guided along the way.

June 10, 2000

A Note from Vee's Journal:

Sean is here spending the weekend as Janet is in a workshop in Los Olivos. He was worried something might happen to her and had trouble getting to sleep. We snuggled in bed, and I rubbed his head for a while and held his tummy. Then we started talking, and the fear left him.

Feeling the joys of my grandson Sean, I can't help but think about my health as my arm signals me today. It often reminds me to care for my body. The physical sensations come and go.

June 11, 2000

A Note from Vee's Journal:

Today Sean and I are going to the theatre at Hearst Castle. They have a display of old camping equipment from the pioneer days. Also, "The Grand Canyon: The Hidden Secrets" is showing at the National Geographic Theatre. It is about remote areas of the canyon with unique views and cascading waterfalls that flow into the Colorado River. The wide-screen is hard for me, but I just look down when it's too much. All in all, it is very educational, and they do such a dramatic job of making it real.

June 12, 2000

A Note from Vee's Journal:

There are times of doubt and times of complete faith. In the times of doubt, I am not questioning the power of God, but rather my confidence in myself. Faith continues to build me up spiritually, physically, and emotionally. I want people to heal and be an example to others. In order to do this, I must hang on to a deep trust.

June 14, 2000

A Letter from Janet's Journal:

Dear Mom,

As I wait for the results of my mammogram to come in, I reflect back on our talk of a week ago. I told you that the technician gave me two breast models, both containing nodules — one benign and the other, malignant. The malignant nodules were very hard. I recall your response vividly. You said, "That is what mine is. It feels like a marble."

I stood up and crossed my front lawn, suddenly feeling the reality of it all. While blips of our conversation ran across my mind, I found myself entering into a new level of acceptance, something I have fought against all of my life. No longer feeling paralyzed in the grips of fear, I realize it is part of the process of letting go. In the past, it had been easy to

throw myself into the denial mode, but I am
beginning to understand denial takes too much
energy.

Your words, "Maybe you will become a
pioneer in changing how our culture deals with
death," keep coming to the forefront of my mind.
Yeah, that would be fine if I could get there first.

So I ask myself – why the fight? Wouldn't it be
much easier to change the way I view death? The
last thing I want to do is prolong your life, especially
if you have done your work and are ready to go on. I
couldn't go there with Auntie Helen. I wasn't able to
let her go.

Bit by bit, little by little, I find myself letting go
of you. It feels good. I would never have been able to
do this or even say that before. I would have felt
morbid admitting it, followed with guilt and shame
for thinking morbid thoughts. Ah...the tangled webs
we weave.

For now, I thank God for being a part of your
life and you a part of mine. I have learned so much.

May you continue to teach me, to bring me new awareness in seeing life through the dying process. May we all forgive each other and learn to come from our hearts. Love you.

June 14, 2000

A Note from Vee's Journal:

This has been some day. I went for my walk as usual, feeling great. I had an appointment with an acupuncturist. I have seen her a couple of times, although she is not my regular one. Well, when she felt the lump in my breast and lymph system, she went on a rampage, saying over and over, "You have to go to a surgeon!" She kept saying, "You have to! I don't want you to die! Acupuncture and herbs will not heal cancer." She left no room for my intuition or my thoughts. I had never been talked to with such force. Well, she did what she thought she had to, but it really shook me up. On the way home, I decided to go see Margaret Butterworth, the minister at Unity Church in Cambria. She gave me back my positive feeling by saying, "No one has the right to tell you what you have to do." We prayed together, and I felt much better. I think my faith will be stronger, and I believe there is more to learn about myself.

Walking on the East West Ranch helped a lot, too. I was sitting on the driftwood bench asking God to speak to me, when all of a sudden I heard a bird singing. I looked toward the sky all around me and couldn't see a bird. It was perched on a pole about one foot above my head. The message was clear. I was not alone. God speaks in many ways.

June 15, 2000

A Note from Vee's Journal:

A blanket of fog covered the early morning. I walked as usual, but could not see the ocean, yet, I knew the ocean waves were there. They are always there. A blanket of fog sometimes covers life, and my faith recedes. But life is always there. When the fog lifts, I am stronger than ever.

June 20, 2000

A Note from Vee's Journal:

This morning I awoke shortly after 3:00. The quiet of the morning hours encourages my inner work. Today, I select a tape by Caroline Casey on astrology. I want to dance with the planets.

Right now it is so easy for me to doubt my own belief system. When money is not coming, I'm afraid. If only I could stand still and listen to the quiet, I would be doing myself a favor. I know it is within me to transcend all negativity. My brain needs a rest. Why not check in with my inner self. I pick up Lucia Capacchione's book, "The Power of Your Other Hand" and decide to write with my non-dominant hand.

Right hand: Why are you feeling a loss of power?

Left hand: It is within your very reach. You are almost there. Your grandfather is an important guide. He will show you the way.

After writing in my journal, I decided to take a short nap. It was 6:00 a.m. and still foggy outside. I chose not to walk yet.

While asleep, I had the most powerful dream. I was in a room similar to a dorm or apartment house. There was a man with me. I don't know if he was a lover or a guide or perhaps just a friend. We were both nude. Suddenly, I heard a jiggling on the lock of the door as if someone were trying to enter. I could hear the key turning back and forth, but nothing was happening. I dressed quickly just in case it was my mother. My friend put on his clothes, although we had nothing to hide. I went to the door and called, "Mother," several times. It could have been my little brother as a child. I called his name, although the name is not clear to me. I sat down in a chair. I was telling my friend, "I just want to be."

All of a sudden, a large figure zoomed through the door. A rather jolly person with loose fitting clothes. It was quite obvious he was there for me and had something to say, but I can't remember what he said. It didn't seem to soak in at the time. He carried so much power. My friend said, "Isn't that what you were just saying? That you just want to be?" It means the same thing.

The figure stood there in emanating power. I was so struck by him, but then he disappeared before my eyes. I cried out, "I can't see you." I believe he appeared and disappeared again. He meant so much to me. After searching outside for him, I went back to my door at the end of the hall, but it was someone else's room. I checked the room next to it, but it wasn't my room either. Going out on the street, I didn't find him. Instead there were neighbors walking with children and dogs. I returned to my waking state feeling a huge change and powerful experience.

June 21, 2000

A Note from Vee's Journal:

This morning I listened to a tape by Carolyn Casey on astrology. The information inspired me to

start a writing class. Perhaps do Reiki on the people
as they enter. I am excited about it. I am comfortable
doing massage, but there is this push from under-
neath to do something else. I am on the Sea of Change,
but not knowing which way the wind will take me.
I must be willing to ride on the waves of the unknown
and dance with the sea.

July 5, 2000

A Note from Vee's Journal:

Yesterday was my first meeting with the
Tuesday prayer group. These compassionate
individuals have been convening every Tuesday for
many years. Sharing inspirational thoughts, they
connect with love, for each other, and the planet.

Athena and Sam from Hawaii were special
guests here on this day to share their healing work.
Sam brought an instrument that resembles a rain stick
called a didgeridoo. I love the sounds that resemble
whales talking or singing to each other.

An amazing thing this morning while lying in bed. Sounds like those from the whale began emerging through my throat. I felt as though I were under water. It felt comfortable and warm.

Today Athena and Sam came by to give me a private session. Athena channeled information as well as her healing touch and vocal sounds. Very lightly she whispered in my right ear, "This dear soul has lived many lifetimes. She has helped many people. She doesn't need to feel responsible for other people's suffering. Her prayers and kindness are enough."

The words Athena spoke combined with the sounds of Sam's didgeridoo filtered through my whole being. I was at peace.

July 14, 2000

A Note from Janet's Journal:

My life is filled with grief. I am exhausted from it. I am tired of it. I wish it all to go away.

Then from deep within, I hear myself saying, "I can do this thing called Life!"

For now, I offer a prayer,

Dear God, I feel like I am pulling out of my deep grieving and the mourning period is about to end. Now what? I get a call from dad, and he informs me that cancer was found in his prostate. He will phone me back to tell me if it has spread elsewhere in his body. How much can one take? Is this where my spirit must come forth and accept the continued onslaught? Must I accept letting go of people close to me, one by one, with no breathers in between? Will I be planning another service? As the tears well up, my soul cries, "No!" Death approaches like the hurricane hitting landfall before its expected time. I'm not good with the unexpected. I have enough trouble with the expected. God, I want to live! I want freedom from my pain. I want to be free, too, of witnessing Sean's pain. Why is it that a seven-year old has to come to grips with his father's death? I fear this grief will kill me! What is it I need to know to bring understanding? To bring peace? Please guide me along my way. Thank You. And so it is.

July 15, 2000

A Note from Janet's Journal:

Good news, yesterday. That other lump my mom found in her breast was an infection. I'm not sure how I would have handled a metastatic cancer.

July 16, 2000

A Note from Vee's Journal:

Tish and John Allan came by on Friday. I wanted to share my story with them. John healed himself of cancer in 1974. As we talked, I explained the three Era's that are described in Larry Dossey's book, "Reinventing Medicine." In Era I, Dossey describes a period of time in which George Washington died of a Strep throat. The medical profession was at a loss in treating his disease. Era II incorporates body/mind techniques, embracing the whole of a person. I explained to Tish and John how much I resonate with Era III, which combines prayer and energy medicine and will one day play an important role in hospital settings. The thought creates a spark within my soul. I set my intention to be a part of this Era.

July 17, 2000

A Note from Vee's Journal:

Warm breezes fanned me stirring up currents of air as I sunbathed on the upstairs deck today. It was as though the angels had decided to join me. I sent out loving thoughts to all people everywhere wishing them the joy of this moment.

July 19, 2000

A Note from Vee's Journal:

A new and exciting day unfolds at this moment. In a few minutes, I will leave for Exotic Nature where Lissa has set up two massage rooms. There I will educate people about Reiki. Who knows if I will have any clients? No matter. My energy will be with the people, and that is important to me. Even though money is needed in my life, I will release that

thought of earning and keep the thought of giving.
The money will take care of itself, or perhaps I should
say, The Universe will. There is so much abundance,
both out there and within, if I tap into it. Be with it.
Breathe it in. Be in the flow of it. Dance with it. Live
it!

Opportunities abound. I am grateful. Recently
new people have come into my life bringing a sense
of newness. No longer am I stuck with and glued to
old patterns and habits. For this I am grateful. My
heart reaches out to all people who want a change in
their lives, but can't seem to move with it.

I repeat a favorite Buddhist quote, "May they
find happiness and the root of happiness, and may
they be free of suffering and the root of suffering."

July 29, 2000
A Note from Vee's Journal:

What a healing session with Timothy! Aura
Chi Integration was something I had never
experienced. It is another version of energy work.

Timothy connected with my energy and pulled it in through his body, sent it down to Mother Earth where it was cleansed and restored and then sent back to me. He worked with sound to release old patterns stuck within the body and psyche.

August 4, 2000
A Note from Vee's Journal:

The view from my studio window is peaceful. Where I usually see a sunset, fog embraces the trees. Not one leaf stirs.

August 6, 2000
A Note from Janet's Journal:

Today, my mom is unencumbered by her faith in God, knowing her faith in God is the same as her faith in herself.

At the same time my intuition comes through. It feels like one of those pivotal points in life, not an epiphany, but a turning point. At such a point, I listen and follow heart. Write the book! It is time to shift into gear and work. Along with work, take time out to enjoy the pleasures of life and of motherhood.

August 7, 2000
A Note from Vee's Journal:

Janet and Sean arrive to spend the night. Tomorrow I will take Sean to view the elephant seals just beyond San Simeon and allow Janet some time alone to study. After lunch, we drove to an area where we thought we could explore the tide pools, but arrived during high tide. Instead, we drove to Ben Franklin's and bought a deck of cards. While playing Slap Jack outside the store, we found the deck to have nine Jacks, so returned it.

August 14, 2000
A Note from Vee's Journal:

After a trip to Mt. Shasta with my friends from Unity, I arrive home shortly after midnight. What a wonderful trip it was! We had all attended the *I Am* pageant. The setting sun created pink clouds over and around the mountain, creating a magnificent backdrop.   A sight to behold!

August 20, 2000

A Note from Janet's Journal:

While driving down the road today I said out loud: "God, I love life sometimes!"

Sean looked at me and said, "You should love it all the time!"

Ah...the lessons we share.

August 21, 2000

A Note from Vee's Journal:

I talked to the moon through my skylight, and in return, it sent a beam of light to me.

~ 8 ~

SUMMER INTO FALL

August 31, 2000

A Note from Janet's Journal:

Today, I witnessed my mom tell her story. We sat together with Maureen Murdock on the outside lawn of Pacifica Graduate Institute. We had both signed up and attended a two-day writing workshop

with Maureen. This was the second day, and
Maureen had invited us to join her for lunch. While
my mom read, I blinked away my tears at a moment's
notice, careful not to intrude. She touched me deeply.
For the first time, I was struck with the enormity of
the anguish and pain she felt in telling her children of
the news of her breast mass. God, this had never
even dawned on me! I was so stuck in my own self-
pity! I was grateful we all took that trip to Idaho. I
will cherish the memories forever.

We left Pacifica and drove into Santa Barbara.
While my mom visited with Jessa, I ran to Borders. My
intuition told me to buy Tristine Rainer's, "Write
Your Story" for my mom.

A Letter from Janet's Journal, *evening entry*:
Dear Mom,

Thank you for sharing not only your news of
the mass, but your sensitivity to me when I was
surrounded by my own grief and pain. I realize now
how difficult this was for you.

Mom, should we write our story together – a mother/daughter journey through breast cancer?

Love you,

Janet

September 2, 2000

A Letter from Janet's Journal:

Dear Mom,

You looked so good to me, which led me to believe you were okay. What I really want to know is that you will be okay when you die. On an intellectual level, this is clear. On an emotional level, it is not.

I want to cry today and don't know why. I think it's a combination: my life and the many challenges that face me and witnessing you the other day as you read your paper to Maureen. I could hear the tears underlying your words, and I could feel mine as they hesitantly began to surface. But I held them at bay, for there was no way I could cry if you didn't. Your anguish over telling your children hit me hard again today. Life is not about me.

Today, as you said you plan to rewrite the story and include the ending just as you would like it to be, I immediately focused my attention on you and your process. What a wonderful idea! Let us write our own endings! Anything is possible!

I love you,

Janet

Hugs…

September 5, 2000

A Note from Janet's Journal:

Sean starts third grade tomorrow. He is ready, except he desperately needs a haircut! He has been cutting his own hair over the summer.

A Letter from Janet's Journal, *evening entry*:

I wish you well on your journey, Mom. I am learning not to interfere. It is hard to let go of loved ones, but I think that gradually I am allowing myself the grace to do so.

I love you very much, Mom

Janet

September 5, 2000

A Note from Vee's Journal:

Today, I am filled with the light. After hearing a tape by Myrtle Fillmore, founder of Unity, my thoughts turn to the God within, knowing that only perfection reigns. It is amazing to me that someone who lived in the late 1890s could be sharing what the healers and writers of today are saying. Myrtle was a lot like my grandmother who held the same belief system. She lived in the same time era. I relate to both of them and find their words comforting as I ask to be healed. This wound in my body was my own doing; therefore it is up to me to undo the obstruction with conscious effort and a knowing that God is in my body and would like perfection.

Today, I am going to San Luis Obispo to renew my driver's license. What a privilege it is to be able to drive. My 73rd birthday is coming soon. I give thanks for each and every day. My life is filled with goodness. Negative thoughts are shooed away as soon as they enter my consciousness.

What a privilege it is to write and heal. Writing creates a healing process and as the healing transforms my thinking, clear insights emerge.

September 11, 2000
A Birthday Wish from Janet's Journal:
"HAPPY BIRTHDAY MOM!"

I'm so glad you are enjoying your day ~ the day you came into the world 73 years ago. "Zen-Out" just like you said to me. Enjoy every moment and every breath. You deserve the best! Enjoy every moment you have here.

Thank you for teaching me so much about life. I know we will be connected throughout eternity.

Mom, I love you with all my heart and soul.

Before closing, I offer a prayer,

Dear God, Thank You so much. I am eternally grateful. Bless my mom today and everyday. May Your love and light fill our beings. I love You with all my heart and soul. May You bless the world today and heal its troubles. And so it is.

September 13, 2000

A Note from Vee's Journal:

Today is Kris's birthday. He will be 21. Bless him and may he receive divine guidance in his life.

I am grateful for the teachings of Myrtle Fillmore. She was blessed with knowledge that has healed many people. I am grateful for my friends, many of whom are healers. I am grateful for prosperity. I am grateful for my children and their support. I am grateful for my body and the wisdom to heal.

I enjoyed my 73rd birthday. I passed my vision and written test for my driver's license, for which I give thanks. Such thoughtful gifts from my family members! Jessa's beautiful card with cheery sunflowers. Justin's Zen Garden from a nature store. Karen's affirmation cards and Clinique moisture lotion. Janet and Sean's gift basket of tea towels, a Buddha, the book "The Rhythm of Compassion" and vibrational chimes.

I woke up to a luminous moon today, subtle and soft. My desire was to be filled with that light. Today brings an opportunity to work at Lissa's. May I have only good in my mind and in my heart today.

September 16, 2000
A Note from Vee's Journal:

Up at 4:00 am with blueberries and cereal, I embark on the day.

The Medicine cards this morning presented Rabbit. This means facing fears. Over the last few days, fears have tried to creep in. I am constantly making affirmations to overcome them. One affirmation in particular that appears often in the Louse Hay affirmation cards is someone walking on a path. The saying is "The point of power is in the present moment."

Gary Zukov says, "'Feel the fear,' and then say to yourself, Do I want this frightened part of myself to make decisions or do I want to have power over it? I choose power right this moment. If I manifest power in my life, that is authentic power."

September 18, 2000
A Letter from Janet's Journal:
Dear Mom,

I eloquently shared your gift of grace with my sisters of The Circle last night. I found I could discuss my experience of acceptance with them. I was strong in articulating it, re-affirming my acceptance.

Thank you for the gift of life and the gift of accepting dying as part of living. May you always be free to live and to move on.

> I love you with all my heart,
>
> Janet

September 22, 2000

A Note from Vee's Journal:

Today is Jessa's 34th birthday. Life is not easy for her. I do hope she becomes a success. She has such talent.

This is the first day of fall Equinox, and with it comes rain.

Janet just phoned to tell me she and Sean will be going to North Carolina to see her father and his wife for Thanksgiving. I am delighted for them.

September 24, 2000

A Note from Vee's Journal:

Night before last I was thinking it would be neat to have a friend just to call and to walk with on the beach.

September 30, 2000

A Note from Vee's Journal:

This is the last day of September. The months are speeding by. I had a wonderful lunch at Bistro

Sole. Nancy had given me a gift certificate for $25, so I blew the whole thing. Crusty Sesame Salmon with Turnips Anna. I don't even like turnips, but they were so disguised by seasonings that I found them delicious. Brought home a lemon tart with whipped cream. I would love to gain back some of the weight I lost with my cleansing diet. Skin and bones was what I was. I remember being only flesh and bones. No flesh on my face – just bones with skin wrapped around it. When I tried on leggings at Leslie Marks Clothing, I looked at my legs in the mirror and ran as fast as I could back to the dressing room before anyone could see me.

Well, now, things are much better. The only thing is my skin is so wrinkled and the muscle tone is gone. But I'm alive!! I believe that when my face looked like a skeleton in the mirror, it revealed a death to my old self and now a new self has emerged. A resurrection. I no longer want to go back to my old way of doing and thinking.

October 2, 2000

A Note from Vee's Journal:

I am thankful to be in God's circle of ever-renewing life. This is a great quote from Unity Magazine today. Daily Word, a publication from Unity Village, has brought me much comfort and kept me in closer contact with God. I used to think my Grandmother Denison was too religious as she practiced constant prayer and teaching of the scriptures. Now, I feel we must have this flow of God's love flowing through us at all times.

Yesterday, I gave Terri, my new neighbor, a treatment of combined massage and energy balancing. After the massage we took three of my watercolors to her house, and I went on to church. When I came home, she had already hung two of them. They bought them. What a joy! It feels good to have someone "fall in love" with your work. I must get started with my artwork again. I have had "time-out" for quite a while. That is okay. That has

happened before. When I start again, my work is
different.

October 5, 2000

A Note from Vee's Journal:

Yesterday I facilitated two workshops, one at
Exotic Nature and the other in my studio. Both went
very well. The theme was "Your Inner Physician"
and how to access it through intuition.

Today I am giving one treatment. I plan to
spend time at the beach and also to clean.

October 6, 2000

A Note from Vee's Journal:

In route to the beach, I took a wrong turn, but
was it really a wrong turn? As I turned around I
heard, "Hi Vee!"

My friend, Judith, was running out of a house.
She approached me and invited me in for a cup of tea,
which I gladly accepted. She made peanut butter
sandwiches for us. Afterwards, we headed for

Moonstone Beach. We sat, and enjoyed the sunset together. So here was an answer to my silent request just nights before. We went back to her house, where she did a reading for me.

I am hoping to be more spontaneous in the future.

October 6, 2000

A "Declaration to God" from Vee's Journal:

I declare that I can actualize a healing for myself with respect to these conditions:

Lump in breast and congestion in lumpy area

Vee Riley   6 Oct. 00

October 13, 2000

A Note from Vee's Journal:

Today is Friday the 13th – a lucky day. Sara and I will leave about 1:30 and go to Los Olivos. We will meet Janet and go to the Labyrinth for a full moon celebration. I made a collage for the occasion. An Indian woman (or man) watching a full moon.

The other day I was walking up a hill on my usual morning walk. After a rain, the sun came out. I didn't see rainbow colors in the street, but my path in front of me was shining purple and gold. It was that way all the way up the hill. The colors alternated. I said, "I am walking in the purple and the gold." What a special gem of a happening.

October 14, 2000

A Note from Janet's Journal:

Having arrived at the church in Los Olivos, I enter the Labyrinth. With each step, I speak my mantra, "I let go. I release." I walk into the middle and choose the first pedal to the left. I stand in it. I begin to pray. Kneeling in the pedal, I continue my prayer. I look up and notice my mom standing directly across from me. Her eyes are closed. I look intently into her face. Her eyes open and are looking up. She is searching for the full moon. She is a child of God. I am blessed that she is my mother, and I give thanks. Our eyes meet, and we smile. We look deeply into one another and clearly our souls meet. We are joined as one in the moment. We smile; even begin to giggle a tiny bit. I force myself not to laugh, as I feel like I could crack up. It doesn't feel like a nervous laugh; it is more of a playful, angelic laugh. I enjoy it and am reminded of our prior rituals, and how we always laugh at some point. She is precious. So precious. I cherish this moment.

Standing, we walk towards each other and embrace. We hold each other gently and lovingly. It feels natural. I feel so much compassion for her and let her know it in my hug — the heart-to-heart hug she taught me. I say in my own heart, it's okay to go on when you are ready. I say this because I know it on another level, and I no longer want to hold her back if she is ready. I bless her. We walk out. I give thanks.

October 17, 2000

A Note from Vee's Journal:

Hey Justin, Happy Birthday! Hope you are continuing with your artwork. I love you!

October 19, 2000

A Note from Vee's Journal:

Last night my "Intuitive Healer" group met. We have only one more class, but we have hardly begun to tap into the unconscious or to establish ways of "knowing". I want to bring the outer and inner parts of myself into harmony.

Two days ago, I went to see a healer in the north county. He lives way out in the country. Lucia told me about him. He feels that we can shrink the tumor in my breast. He used Moxa on certain acupressure points along with an electrical unit that works like Acupuncture, but does not puncture the skin. He is also experienced with Kirilian photography. Only the fingertips are photographed. He goes over this information with his own intuitive feelings and comes up with a diagnosis. He said my heart gave the indication it was tired. I also had a weak pulse throughout my body. He doesn't take the pulse on the wrist like most doctors but rather the full body pulse. He checks the heart rate from under the arm instead of a stethoscope.

Detoxification for two weeks was suggested. I had never done this before. I must say it feels good to clean out the intestines. Another treatment is asparagus extract in the form of a tea. It actually tastes good. A capsule of Maitake mushroom was also recommended. I like him.

October 21, 2000
A Note from Janet's Journal:

In the stillness and quiet of a new day, amidst an often-times perilous journey, I step forward knowing that all is well in my world. I pray for the sick, the confused, the hurting, all those who are hungry, and for those who are abused.

October 22, 2000
A Note from Vee's Journal:

Today, I got up at 3:30 a.m. Ate breakfast while listening to Myrtle Fillmore tape -- went back to bed on the couch. Had some interesting dreams, which are vague in my mind, but awoke with "paintings of people" as vivid words. I took that as my message from the subconscious. So I will paint people.

I have been thinking about what a healer said about my not wanting to lose control of my situation. That is partly due to the medical field and a strong belief that they do so much damage to people. I will soften and open to wisdom. I can still make choices and be in charge of my own health and know at the same time that I do need help in this. God the creator is my main source of help, but I have asked Him to put me in touch with the right people. This, as I see it, is an answer to my prayer to God. This is part of my personal growth. When I allow myself to soften and be open, so too shall the lump in my breast.

At the same time I must hold on to my power and speak my truth.

October 24, 2000

A Letter from Janet's Journal:

Dear God,

I need this time to reflect. I am realizing that all my hard work needs balance. A time to reflect, to just BE. How can I do all of this? Doesn't everybody dream of the day when they can sit in the warm sun in their gardens, listening to the wild calls of birds, meditating, reflecting, finding peace and harmony? Restoring the soul? Soul work is difficult and needs this time. So today I do what it takes. There is plenty of time for me to write. All of my school papers will get in on time. I am open and willing. I am grateful for this time. Thank you. I will live my life by paying it forward. And so it is.

A Note from Janet's Journal, *evening entry*:

After a free-write exercise, a journal entry. I know that when I suppress my innermost feelings, I become anxious, confused, and even sick.

October 28, 2000

A Note from Vee's Journal:

Today, I am encouraged to remove the lump in my breast. The naturopath came to Cambria to give me my second treatment. He was so pleased that my body pulse was so much better. He will try and get rid of the lump by two methods. One, he would hold it with two fingers and the other was some kind of machine he used on it. When he was holding it with two fingers, I thought, why haven't I been able to get rid of it since I have done Reiki on it. Then I thought of Christ who said, "When two or three are gathered together in my name, there will I be also." Maybe that makes a difference. He said he could feel it changing. When I looked in the mirror afterward, I felt it had changed. I like the diet he put me on to gain weight. It is important that I continue with the treatment. He has offered to treat me for free if money is an issue.

November 10, 2000

A Note from Vee's Journal:

John, my children's father, called this morning to say he was cancer free!

November 18, 2000

A Letter from Janet's Journal:

Dear God,

I feel as though I'm being stripped down to nothing. But I know there is something – it's more like I'm being stripped down to something, to my core – to my soul. Nothing can harm my soul.

~ 9 ~

TELLING OTHERS AND AN ACTIVE MIND

November 23, 2000

A Note from Vee's Journal:

    I went through a change as far as the lump in my breast. Decided to tell a few people. Thought maybe that would help. I am not sure that it did. It's like there is more focus on it. I'm feeling okay about it now, but the last week brought about some fears. The more people involved, the more fear is created. I just want to feel that my own intuition is guiding me along with God. Or is it one and the same?

John at Unity grabbed me up and gave me a little lecture on Sunday. Fifteen years ago he had tumors all through his body. He said if the tumors are not in your mind, they will not be there. So have I been paying too much attention to my condition? That is my question.

My naturopath invited me for Thanksgiving dinner so maybe that is my answer. I was wondering if the treatments should be continued. I will see him tomorrow for a regular diet.

News Flash! I just heard from Janet. What a frightening experience! She and Sean were in the Charlotte, North Carolina International Airport when someone went through security with a gun. They, along with 3000 others, were held in a confined, secured area while they searched the airport.

Everyone was a nervous wreck. She has just phoned me from her dad's car.

November 24, 2000
A Note from Vee's Journal:

Stayed home for Thanksgiving. All went well with only Jessa here. The turkey breast and all that goes with it was divine. Jessa went hiking while I put the turkey in the oven. We ate at 3 pm. Took Mabel, my neighbor, a plate of food.

Have been trying to calm my mind about my lymph condition. It flares up every once in a while, and I don't know if my mind becomes too active because of it or if it flares up because my mind is too active.

This morning I was feeling sorry for myself, and after meditating, I started appreciating the day and experienced an immediate mind shift. Went for a walk and thanked my lucky stars for all my good.

Jay Powels CD and Hannah's guided meditations have been a great inspiration to me.

December 4, 2000

A Note from Vee's Journal:

Sean came to visit me over the weekend. Janet went to a very intense workshop. I took Sean to the National Geographic theatre at Hearst Castle, and we watched the documentary on Egypt. We went to lunch afterwards.

Sunday, Sean and I went to the beach to honor his Grandfather Mauk with some rose petals at Moonstone Beach. Home to roast marshmallows in the fireplace.

Last week I visited my naturopath. He has helped me in a lot of ways, but the lump is still there. He feels it is in the lymph system. He thought he could shrink it, but it's not happening. It is a fairly good-sized tumor, but the tissue around it is much better than it was a year ago. It doesn't bother me to drive anymore and, it doesn't get sore if I over-do. I must constantly seek answers as to what to do about it. The challenge has provided room for much growth, for which I am grateful. I wish it would leave my body but it may never bother me. I plan a happy ending to my life!

December 9, 2000

A Letter from Janet's Journal:

Dear Mom,

Grandpa Mauk died a little over a week ago on December 1. In his passing, he brought me truly wondrous gifts, and I am blessed. Thank you, Grandpa Mauk, I am eternally grateful. I love you!

Mom, I feel as though the San Francisco trip is our last trip together. It is in one week and I so look forward to it. In a way it is not difficult – this knowing. In another, it is most difficult. On a soul level it is wondrous, pure bliss, pure love, pure acceptance. On a physical level it is pure anguish, pure pain, a heartache that can only be described as ineffable pain. A pain that must be felt.

Freedom is in the letting go. Once we let go of everything – all the material things, all attachments, we are FREE. I had a taste of this, and I desire more.

I think about the quote from Aronie, "The real power is not about control, but about letting go."

I love you Mom with all my heart – you are free to move on. Bless you. Love you always.

December 10, 2000

A Note from Vee's Journal:

I am so grateful for this day. The clouds and sky are magnificent. Church met at Margaret's house. It is a time of sharing. People talked about the synchronicity in our lives, and how God works. The stories were both sad and funny. I didn't talk – just listened, but it was very meaningful. Tish and John are such great people.

The moon tonight is almost full. Tomorrow night it will be. It reminded me of how grateful I am!

December 15, 2000

A Note from Vee's Journal:

I have been listening to Deepak Chopra "Magical Mind, Magical Body." Great insights! If you want to heal an area in your body, replace the memories of that condition. Transcend any fear and doubt. I have been thinking of this lump in my body as hard and stationary. My thinking will change to soft and fluid. The memories that caused the condition are still there. I have already done some healing techniques to improve my condition, but I need to do more.

Just when I think the lump has served its purpose, I think again. The cells in my body are constantly changing. Moving – like the ocean waves. A year ago, it hurt to shift gears in my car. It hurt to carry wood. If I moved a certain way, it hurt. That is no longer true.

December 16, 2000

A Letter from Janet's Journal:

Dear Mom,

I awaken to Celine Dion's Christmas CD. You walk down the hallway and say, "Are you guys up?"

You said you were meditating and heard music and thought the angels were singing to you. I love it.

Well, we leave for San Francisco today. I'm excited and nervous about it. I actually wonder if I will ever be able to travel again without fear. I have no idea really when this all began, but it seems to be there – some underlying monster that won't go away. Mostly I think I feel like I am not going to make it!

In any event, today I choose to be "Dorothy." Yesterday, I was lying on the massage table, and Louise and I were talking. She said something about changing my name or being someone else for the weekend, leaving behind everything I need to forget about. "Dorothy" quickly slipped into my mind. Louise mentioned that she was reminded of Dorothy in the Wizard of Oz. A perfect metaphor! I definitely feel as though I am being taken on a ride. So yes...I'm definitely ready for the land of enchantment. Could it be San Francisco, or is this just the beginning? I will wait and see. I affirm: For now, I go to San Francisco fearlessly. I am filled with joy every minute we are there. I travel with confidence knowing I am healthy and safe where I am. And so it is.

Thank you, Mom, for wanting to pass the Christmas season in San Francisco down to Sean. I will write about it. I will also consider a chapter on "Being Dorothy for a Weekend in San Francisco."

I love you. Enjoy.

Janet

A Note from Janet's Journal during flight to San Francisco, *same day*:

Mom writes in my journal during our flight to San Francisco. I read it over and over and over. I am swirling in the depths of the underworld. Nothing can lift me from this place. She writes a Unity prayer.

I lay my every thought before You, God
The love of God protects me
The light of God surrounds me
Free my mind
I am at peace, knowing the presence of God is with
me at all times.

Silently I give thanks, smile in her direction, and pray this recent depression lifts soon.

December 22, 2000

A Note from Janet's Journal:

I sit alone. Truly, I feel alone. I can't feel You, God. Your presence is absent. I can't feel my guide's presence. I find myself saying, God, help me. Nothing changes. I feel down, so down. I also think this will be my last Christmas with my mom. Shit, I can't even imagine this for a moment! Dorothy! I need Dorothy!

December 28, 2000

A Note from Vee's Journal:

It has been awhile since picking up this journal. On December 16 Janet, Sean and I went to San Francisco. Jessa took us to the airport in Santa Barbara. All transportation went smoothly from beginning to end, including cable cars, buses, and taxis. We stayed in a Bed and Breakfast out by

Golden Gate Park. Very nice. Sean and I had waffles every morning. On Saturday, Dorothy covered Nordstrom's, Union Square, Ghirardelli Square, and rode home by taxi.

Sunday we went to Grace Cathedral for the Holy Eucharist. I was surprised at the openness of the Episcopal Church now. Even I was allowed to receive communion after not attending a service for thirty years. Eight-year-old Sean also was allowed to partake. What a change!

Sunday after church we went by cable car to the Hard Rock Café, and as usual Janet, aka Dorothy, and I danced our way to the booth. Then on to the Academy of Science at Golden Gate Park. By then, it was about 2:30, and we didn't have time to cover everything. We went back the next day. Janet's friend is a docent there and took us on a private tour. Back on the plane, we landed in Santa Barbara about 5:00 pm. Jessa was there to meet us. The next day there were lots of delays in travel. Were we lucky!!

The following weekend was Christmas. I went to Solvang again on Saturday. Sunday was Christmas Eve. We had a beautiful dinner, which Janet wanted to cook all by herself. Opened presents after, since Sean could hardly wait. All my family went together and gave me an E-mail Station. The lines have been so busy because of the Christmas rush; I could not get through to activate it. Decided to call at 6:00 a.m. and it worked. It has been activated, although I must wait forty-eight hours before I can use it. Looking forward to email.

December 31, 2000
A Note from Janet's Journal:

One year ago, December 31, 1999, I wrote the following journal entry: *I am willing. I am loving. I open my heart. I have the courage I need to face and learn my lessons. I'm ready for whatever comes.*

Today, my response is a cynical laugh. Reflecting back, I was willing, although at times, resistant. I was loving, although at times resistant.

Courageous, yes. Whenever I have needed courage, I have asked, and courage has been granted. Always!

What a year this has been! A roller coaster ride! But I'm learning, and what more could I ask for?

On January 3rd of this year, I had asked to be open. I was willing to change. And I had specifically written: I'm ready for whatever comes. Little did I dream what was coming. The phone call from my mother changed my life, the way I lived it, and the way I viewed it.

I close this year with gratitude. While not wanting to live it over, I treasure all of it. Every experience afforded me new gains and above all, another step closer to acceptance. As the year comes to an end, I am optimistic and hopeful. Again, I remain open to whatever awaits me.

December 31, 2000

A Note from Vee's Journal:

The Eve of the Year 2001

Candle burning, pen in hand, I write: The dying year, slowly fading into midnight, is not afraid. The earth, a mighty foundation, supports humankind in our collective dreams for tomorrow.

Reflecting on the past year, I am reminded of the cycles that come and go. Interchanging, they create impermanence.

The wind chimes on my back porch do not resist the wind. Why then, does my mind traverse with such a struggle? The signals lie before me, waiting to be observed, only to find the Ego clouding my experience with false hopes and actions.

On the other hand, a polarity shift can occur unexpectantly within the innermost core of my being. This deep-seated peace cannot be named. Dis-ease encased in my body has forced me to stop and allow regeneration to occur. On this New Year's Eve, I give thanks for the knowledge my illness has brought me and the lessons that might not have otherwise been learned.

Tonight is a prelude to a fresh new beginning. Arms open, I am ready to embrace the whole of creation and the rhythm of cycles it may bring.

Cheers!

~ 10 ~

SEEKING NEW BEGINNINGS

January 1, 2001

A Letter from Vee's Journal:

Dear God,

At Christmas, I was gifted with another journal. This one is dedicated to You in whom I will reveal my most personal thoughts and desires. I will make this a special ritual and will always use my pink pen. The year ahead flashes before me with uncertainty. Knowing that all things are possible through You, I extend our partnership.

My path lies before me with untrodden footsteps. May each footprint leave behind a sense of knowing along the trail. I seek to take abundant strides on this pilgrimage into Self. I am still growing. Whatever is in store for me in the year 2001, <u>I Can Do It!</u> With Your Benevolent Hand, please guide me as I press on in this exploration of my own unique truth.

Your Child.

January 1, 2001

A Letter from Janet's Journal:

Dear God,

At the beginning of this new year, I ask for a change of heart. May my communion with You grow, minute-by-minute, moment-by-moment. I am forever grateful for Your abiding love, guiding support, and the miracles You create. Thank You.

January 2, 2001

A Letter from Janet's Journal:

Dear Mom,

You have never looked so good! I can't believe it. It's truly remarkable. I do believe in miracles.

I loved going to church with you yesterday. Tish and John had a wonderful message. I could relate to the part about how easy it is to separate our pain and grief from our joy. The metaphor about the river was fabulous. How it all ran together, merging at times of tumultuous undercurrents. Beautiful!

I realize that is exactly what I have done in my life, too. I have separated everything out, actually believing that I couldn't possibly feel joy amidst my pain. Even to the point where I have been defiant and wouldn't allow joy to enter. Wow! I thank you, Tish and John, for this insight.

I felt compelled to do the Inspiration there at your church and followed up by speaking to John. I am on for the second Sunday in February! I have no idea what is going to happen, but I feel a strong desire to speak on "Forgiveness." I send a heartfelt thank you to Grandpa Mauk and invite him to help me with my inspiration. Forgiveness *is* the key.

Thank you, Mom, for leading me to Unity Church in Cambria. I wish you a wonderful year filled with joy.

I love you very much,

Janet

January 2, 2001

An Email to Janet from Vee:

It was such a delight having you and Sean spend New Year's Eve and Day with me. I am so proud of both of you. We have had some good times recently. This is the eighth day of Christmas. I quote from Unity Christmas 2000 as I focus on will. "There are many material things I may wish to obtain or successes I hope to accomplish. I may feel certain that I know what is best for me in my life. The greater truth is that only God knows what is best. It is fine to hold on to my dreams, but not with a firm grasp, for God may have something better in mind for me."

Let me know how the little mother, Binky, is doing.
How many eggs in her nest now?

Sending reams of love.
Mom

January 3, 2001

A Note from Vee's Journal:

Christmas and New Year's have come and
gone. Now only memories. Good memories.
Christmas at Janet's and New Year's here in Cambria.
On New Year's Eve, Janet, Sean and I watched *I
Dreamed of Africa*, a good movie that took us out of
our daily routine. Sad, but wonderful lessons.

Tonight, I will give my first workshop of the
year based on Gail Straub's book. *The Rhythm of
Compassion*. It is about caring for Self while
connecting with society. I was up at 4:00 a.m. in order
to prepare.

January 5, 2001

An Email to Janet from Vee:

I forgot where I read these words, but they made an impact on me. They are: You have let Spirit guide you to seek opportunities, mentors, and education. May the spark of Divinity within you ignite a flame in your heart and give you confidence. Let your gift shine for all the world to see. I love you and have faith in you.

Mom

January 10, 2001

A Letter from Janet's Journal:

Dear God,

There is a void now, but also a knowing. A time of stillness. Deep stillness. A shifting...

"The tears you shed when the ego finally loosens its clutches will never come to anyone else's attention. It happens in the privacy of your heart, in the deep stillness. This is when you drown in love. This is the cleansing bath. This is going naked before God. This is deep communion with God."

__ Gurumayi Chidvilasananda

January 16, 2001

A Note from Vee's Journal:

It was so cold this morning I didn't go for my walk. Focused on paying all my bills instead. That felt good. I am so grateful to have the money in the bank to pay them. My needs are always met, although it gets scary at times. It definitely is a lesson in trust.

Olivia and I are exchanging massages today. This is the first time. I'm so grateful to have my body fill out. For a while, I was wrinkled skin on bones. This process of healing has been transforming - an opening or gateway to spiritual healing.

My workshop based on the book, *Rhythm of Compassion*, went well. Passed the Kleenex box around. Emotions ran deep.

January 17, 2001

An Email to Janet from Vee, 5:08 a.m.

I respect your time for retreating. Do not feel you need to answer all of my emails. When we detach, it does not mean cool indifference. We can love without expecting anything in return.

This message is for Sean. I am so sorry you have been ill, Sean. Hug yourself and pretend it is from Grammy. A thousand email hugs and kisses are coming your way from Cambria.

January 22, 2001

A Note from Vee's Journal:

Yesterday, I discovered Woodhaven, a retreat center on five acres in Nipomo. I feel at home there. There are no employees, only volunteers. The service began with a meditation in the Nendo room. A woman dressed in a black robe enters and sits facing the group. After thirty minutes of silent meditation, she spoke for about fifteen minutes and then opened the session for discussion.

Afterward she sat and talked with Abby, Ruth, and myself. As she looked at me, she said, "You remind me of an old friend and I think of you as a non-Zen Zen teacher."

I replied, "I am not a Zen teacher, but I am very Zen." I hope to go there again as I was inspired. So many new opportunities have come my way during my healing process. I am grateful.

January 22, 2001

A Note from Janet's Journal:

Have just created a most inviting writing space for the Divine to move through me. I love it at this small table just in front of my bedroom window. The day is clear, affording a most magnificent view of the mountains. The pink roses on my writing table are beginning to open. Beautiful, simple, and delicate. So is life.

I think about the dream I had last night where Sid came to me. It was as though he were giving me permission to write.

So, I say to myself, Janet, as you continue seeking a higher spiritual life, continue to write. Writing keeps you grounded and on your path. We don't always like the path we are on, but always know that where the path leads is to the wonder, the joy, the ecstasy, and to communion with God. That is the ultimate.

January 23, 2001

A Note from Janet's Journal:

The morning sky is stunning. I watch in awe, knowing that today's dawn is the only one of its kind. There will be others, perhaps similar, but none that reveal today's offering. The wonder of sunrises and sunsets, each unique. God's glory displayed for all to see. In these moments, I touch God and God touches me.

January 24, 2001

An Email to Janet from Vee, 6:51 a.m.

I am always open to traveling with you and Sean. Thanks for the invitation. Montana is a place I have not visited. Maybe we could rope a couple of cowboys. Sounds great!

Good luck on your career. You said it was scary. Oprah had a good tip on that. For thirty days write in your journal "What am I afraid of?" If you do it every day, it should reveal some truths.

I am looking forward to Jerry's visit. After many years, I have learned to love my sister unconditionally. It is freeing!

Toodles, Mom

January 24, 2001

A Note from Janet's Journal:

> Happy Birthday to my dad!

> I will spend the day writing. My writing is taking off, and there is a knowing with it. I'm onto something new. So what burden do I need to release in order to birth it? Stirring and building energy, deeply rooted, from my innermost creative place. A force so strong, nothing can stand in its way.

> Amazing how I awoke this morning so alive, and now I just want to die. What is happening? It feels like a death, my own.

Received a beautiful card from my mom and I place it on my writing table. It reads:

Awareness, Service, Peace, Love. In healing the planet, we heal ourselves. Her note inside says, "Every moment is a blessing. There are blessings ahead for you, so just keep on going and keep on growing. Mom

Mom, you are a blessing. You are God's grace in action. I thank God for this blessing, this awareness, this love, this Divine answer to my pain and anguish, to my doubts and fears. As usual, synchronicity happens.

Thank you, Mom!

January 25, 2001

A Note from Janet's Journal:

On days like this, I feel humble. I woke up this morning in a warm bed and warm house. I went to Sean's room and snuggled with him. I am so grateful.

Dropped Sean off at school. On the way back home, I glanced out of my passenger window and saw the most beautiful rainbow. Oh, how I wished

Sean were with me. Perhaps he is viewing it from the schoolyard. I hope so. I pulled forward through the stop sign and looked again. It was following alongside me. I passed the buildings and looked again. It moved with me through the acre parcel just to my right and then up on the hill beyond. I smiled and then started to laugh. I loved it. Suddenly it turned into a double rainbow, and they were both moving with me across the hills and over the cows grazing in the pastures. They actually crossed over the cows!

I will speak my Truth today and love unconditionally.

I look forward to lunch with Aunt Jerry and Uncle Paul.

God, I am thankful.

January 27, 2001

A Note from Janet's Journal:

It's Saturday morning and a freshly snow-capped Figueroa Mountain stands tall, beckoning me forth. I'm tempted.

January 29, 2001

A Letter from Vee's Journal:

Dear God,

Tripped on my own ego. Giving massage to two people, one of them a very muscular man, was a little too much. It was definitely a lesson in controlling or trying to have it my way. I love making people feel good, but to do the healing work, I must take myself out of it, and You, dear God, do the work. I am *yielding* to You and to the Divine within me.

The *NOW* moment is what I want in my life. It is so easy to become caught up in the future outcome of a situation. If only I could stay in the NOW. My experience yesterday must be erased from my mind as having been something done wrong. It caused me to shift my thinking and to stop trying to be all things to all people.

I accept this reality with gratitude. All that is necessary is to know that Divine Order is taking place in my life.   My Soul.

January 30, 2001

A Note from Janet's Journal:

Happy Birthday, Sean! I love you so so much!

Read something profound today. Reading has helped me through this time of uncertainty.

"You do not have a choice about your personal history. But you can choose from your history those things which will lead you to a deeper relationship with your true nature."

_Phillip Moffitt, *The Language of the Soft Heart*

Profound, eloquent, timely, wondrous!

January 31, 2001

A Note from Janet's Journal:

I am letting go of things in my life that no longer serve me, taking a giant leap as though crossing the bridge between the past and present. Material things that I have clutched in a death grip, I lovingly let them go.

I sit down for a splendid lunch, give thanks, and celebrate the wisdom showered upon me today. I thank God. And so it is.

February 2, 2001

A Note from Janet's Journal:

I ended up in the Emergency Room for the night! Doctors ruled out a heart attack. It became very clear to me that there was a profound lesson being offered, one on giving and receiving. Never underestimate the power of God to work through us. I'm certain there is more to this than I'm aware of. The magic is knowing that if I remain open and

willing, something else may come. For now, I can
and will forge on in this journey called LIFE.

February 2, 2001

An Email to Janet from Vee:

This is from one of my Unity magazines:

*"Just for today, O God, grant me the gift of courage so that
I may walk life's pathway free and unafraid and meet each
day's tasks with a courageous heart."*

Love, Mom

February 4, 2001

A Letter from Janet's Journal:

Dear Mom,

I send you blessings as you present the
morning's "Inspirational" at Unity Church of
Cambria. May you find courage and strength. I
know firsthand how difficult it can be to stand before
a group and speak. I also know how easy and

enjoyable it can be. May your gentle spirit shine upon all present.

After my experience the other night in the E.R. I am considering doing my Inspirational on the 18th on receiving. I read the following in *Unity Daily Word* dated January 21, 2001:

"Sacred Commitment. How good it feels to be able to help others. Whenever I am considerate of others and lend a helping hand, I am fulfilling a sacred commitment to be an instrument of God's love."

I wish you well today and everyday.

Loving you!

Janet

February 5, 2001

A Letter from Vee's Journal:

Dear God,

Yesterday, I gave the Inspirational on healing at Unity Church. I felt at home speaking to the group.

Could it be that more talks are on the way, and that this is my calling?

Early in life I was planning to be a foreign missionary and attended William Jewel College with that in mind. My life took another turn. I do not regret my marriage to a clergyman and I am grateful for my three children. All have contributed to my being where I am at this moment.

It is my hope to be an example for others by letting my light shine, letting people know that there are many ways of healing. Only my soul knows the steps I am to take. Your guidance is always available if I but trust. My body can be whole with Your Presence. Thank You, God.

My Soul.

February 7, 2001

A Letter from Janet's Journal:

Today I make no promises except to continue to believe in myself, my work, my wish to seek truth, and my willingness to live in humility and be truly who I am. May *I* radiate into the world and shine upon others so that they may trust in their process to be who *they* really are.

I begin anew today. I am open and willing to create change in my life. I am aware that, at this very moment, change is happening. May my newly acquired awareness bring insight and hope into my life.

Thank You, God, for my life. I deeply appreciate everything I have. Thank you, my mentor and friend, Janet Lucy! Thank you for trusting me, having faith in me, believing in me, honoring me, encouraging me, guiding me, listening, and most importantly in listening - *hearing* me. I rejoice in my authentic being.

February 12, 2001
A Note from Janet's Journal:

A gentle rain taps against the windowpane.

February 13, 2001

A Note from Janet's Journal:

Dealing with so many issues, conflicting feelings, and impossible demands, pulls me in every direction. I need a conversation with God and I will ask for clarity.

February 14, 2001

A Letter from Vee's Journal:

Dear God,

I love You on this Valentine's Day as I love You each day of the year. For the rest of my life, I must and will affirm my good health through You and with You. You are my Strength and my Redeemer. Allow me to have full knowingness of this.

It is beautiful after the rains. I am happy. I feel the joy that accompanies suffering.

Sharing this God Energy with several women from Lucia Capacchione's workshop bathes me in a feeling of gratitude. I know You are within me in all that I do. "Wherever I am, God is," is my mantra. May I continue to follow in the path I have chosen with guidance through my higher self.

My Soul.

February 14, 2001

A Note from Janet's Journal:

Happy Valentines Day to me. It's cool. One more year goes by, and Sean remains my special Valentine. The mountains are loaded with snow. After school today, I'm surprising Sean with a trip there. Can't wait!

I offer a prayer,

Thank You, God, for everything I have and everything coming my way. I am grateful for my experiences and trust I am exactly where I need to be. I love You with all my heart.

February 16, 2001

A Letter from Janet's Journal:

Dear Mom,

After hanging up the phone last night, Sean and I ate dinner and watched a movie. Later, climbing the stairs to my bedroom, I reflected on what you had said earlier. I mulled over the conversation that we had discussed about my attending the Jung Society meeting in San Luis Obispo. I had asked if you wanted to attend the meeting or would you want to watch Sean? Then you had said, "I would love to take care of Sean but I am unable to drive that far."

The words stung. I thought, Wow, that's only forty minutes. Then you said, "The lump is bothering me more, and I don't want to aggravate it."

Entering my room, I lit my lavender candles before reaching for my pajamas. Then it hit me! Oh dear God, what if you die soon? The realization overwhelmed me. I went up and down with it. One minute, I denied the possibility of your death and was relieved that you were doing so well. Then I found myself in the throes of fear, plunged back to last night's phone conversation. Moments of relief and peace came when I knew you were all right, when the Grace of God had provided a reprieve. I appreciated those times and was grateful. But I couldn't stay there and would become fraught with fear. Why is it so difficult to let go?

Early in the day, I picked up my sand tray, raked the sand, and gently placed the glass monk in the center. Closing my eyes, I reached for the plate of rocks. My right hand gently caressed the smooth surfaces. One in particular found its way to my fingertips. I slowly picked it up, opened my eyes, and read the words, *"Make It Happen."* The power of the words struck me, and I knew they were meant for me. All morning, I had been saying to myself, Write the book! I said the words aloud as I wrote them down.

Make It Happen!

I was aware of the paradox. On one hand, I asked for and received God's guidance. I released my life to God. On the other hand, I knew that I was the one who must take action; I must tap my inner power. It was up to me to make it happen. This paradox held no conflict and felt comfortable.

The conflict I felt about your dying consumed me. Mom, I ask one thing of you. Show me the joy in passing over. I know it is there. I know it is possible. Grandpa Mauk showed me and shared with me the joy in dying. Grandpa Mauk and I celebrated; we held a private ceremony. We were both so happy, so joyous, and so in the moment. Nothing else concerned us.

I want to go there with you and to share your experience fully. I want to be joyous. A celebration. But I am not joyous. I ask God to help me transcend my fear, yet a part of me cries out, "I can't live without you!" Another part knows that I will live eternally connected with you though your physical being won't be here. A part of me knows that you will reveal yourself to me in nature. But in me, I am afraid. That fear rocks the core of me. I pray for peace and acceptance and it does not come.

For now, I will *Make It Happen*. You are my inspiration.

My love for you is always,

Janet

February 16, 2001, *same day*:

Another Letter from Janet's Journal:

Dear God,

Show me the way. Thank You for all of it now--ahead of time. I am grateful for everything I have. Please know that!

February 17, 2001

A Letter from Janet's Journal:

Dear Mom,

I continue to love you with all my heart. May you be blessed with Divine moments of Grace along your journey. May the animal kingdom continue to gift you with their presence. May all those who come into your life share your loving presence and light of God.

Always loving you and wishing you well!

Janet

I cry myself to sleep.

February 23, 2001

A Note from Janet's Journal:

I woke up in the night from rain pitter-pattering on the skylight and felt compelled to write. This had not happened for quite some time, and I thought perhaps I had lost the desire entirely.

Now the sun rises somewhere above the stormy sky. The birds sing outside my window. God sings. I will not give up hope. I keep my faith. I am exactly where I need to be.

A Letter from Janet's Journal, *same day*:

Dear God,

I trust in the process of life and know only good comes my way. May I share and teach others Your way. May I always love unconditionally.

I plant a seed of love during this New Moon. I ask for Your guiding light to nurture it, to make this love grow and touch the heart of others.

P. S. Janet, continue to believe in yourself!

February 25, 2001

A Letter from Vee's Journal:

Dear God,

I have been somewhat puzzled about the food I eat. Watching my diet is important to me. At the beginning of the year 2000, I went on a cleansing diet and lost more than seemed right. Little by little, I have gained and feel comfortable once again. Lately, I have felt it was all right to eat sweets once in awhile, however, the lump in my breast seems to be getting bigger. It could be my imagination. I really want to know. Does my diet make that much difference? I feel great and as healthy as anyone could hope to be.

Please let me know why I still have the lump? I will be listening.

My Mind.

I need help, God.

My Soul.

February 26, 2001

A Letter from Janet's Journal:

Dear God,

Continue to guide me, please. I will listen. Guide me and send <u>all</u> of my spirit guides to help me. May I be a vehicle for Your love and light. Your grace in action. May my ears be open. May my mind relax in order to hear You. I ask that you keep Sean safe always. I sit in the quiet, and close my eyes.

The rooster crows up on the hill. The birds sing. Grady's tail thumps the carpet with a happy wag.

February 27, 2001

A Letter from Janet's Journal:

Dear Mom,

I just received your package. Thank you. As I opened it, I thought about how nice it was to receive something from you. The tape of my "Inspirational" and the film canister, both treasures. The thought brushes my mind. I will miss opening packages from you. One day, they will stop, but other kinds of packages will be sent - from you to me. They will be different, but gifts nonetheless.

I am frightened right now. Everything to do with finances and loans, including student aide, is being denied. I wonder why? I will keep my chin up and believe that something else is coming my way.

I love you, Janet

March 1, 2001

An Email to Janet from Vee, 4:19 a.m.

Our Tuesday group is studying the Unity book, 40 Days of Lent. I am really getting into it. Today is dedicated to flexing my spiritual wings, and before I got out of bed, my arms started flying.

Enjoy your time with Dad and Jan.

Abby, my friend, who is moving to Arizona, says she'll be back. We walked on Moonstone Beach at nine this morning. I will miss her.

Toodles, Mom

March 3, 2001

A Note from Janet's Journal:

Disappointment weaves its way through my life. My secret to living through it, is finding solace. Whenever my thoughts are negative, I will let them go. There are so many stages or layers to healing.

Glancing out of my bedroom window, I pause to reflect. A large, silky, black crow comes into view. He sits atop my neighbor's rooftop. It seems he is staring at me. He caws with determination as if he is trying to tell me something. Suddenly he flies directly at me, his wings fully extended, gliding. I thought he was going to fly right into my window but instead, he flew upward at the very last minute. It was beautiful.

Going out into my garden, I begin weeding. Some of the weeds are resistant. Some pull up easily. For others I need the shovel. I reflect upon this metaphor. Thoughts drifted to those people in my life who were and are resistant to change. Myself included. I kept weeding, knowing that two things were happening. I cleared away that which no longer served my garden and made room for new growth. Simultaneously I weeded out my mind, leaving space for me to grow.

Unity's Daily Word prayer for today:

"I lift my thoughts to God and find a spiritual garden within my heart. In times of prayer, I clear out the weeds - negative thoughts or habits and feelings of unforgiveness that have grown up over time - so that I can recognize the blessings which await me."

Loved finding this after spending the day in the garden. So recognize your blessings, Janet. Recognize them!

March 4, 2001

A Note from Janet's Journal:

Water poured from the heavens. The blustering winds raced, sending rain sideways through time and space. The trees whipped fiercely. No birds out today. I prayed for them tucked inside the dancing trees. I missed them and hoped they were safe.

March 5, 2001

A Letter from Janet's Journal:

Dear God,

I am barely hanging on. "Leap and the net will appear." Do I leap? Or have I already? Am I once again in the descent into the underworld of madness and depression? The place to transform pain and confusion to a place of comfort and clarity. Where am I? I want to know. My efforts to deal with life seem wasted. Hope abandons me.

March 7, 2001

A Note from Janet's Journal:

> I awakened in the night. A very clear message came to me. *"It is through the silence, you will know!"*

March 10, 2001

An Email to Janet from Vee, 3:30 a.m.

When Maya Angelo sang "This little light of mine, I'm gonna let it shine" she touched the lives of many. The second verse to that is "Hide it under a bushel, NO, I'm gonna let it shine"! It seems to me you are keeping yours IN A BUSHEL. You know the one, that bushel basket under your writing table over-flowing with creativity? Take a risk and share those stories! I know it is hard to expose one's inner self as, I, too, am still working on that, but if we are to let our lights shine, it takes DOING.

Just a thought with love, Mom

> *"Whatever you think you can do or believe you can do, begin it. Action has magic, grace, and power in it."*
> ___Goethe

March 10, 2001

A Note from Janet's Journal:

Someone said last night, "When you believe in God, amazing things happen." Today, I think I will construct an out-box for God. My inner critic seems to be coming on board - LOUD AND CLEAR!

March 12, 2001

An Email to Janet from Vee, 4:03 a.m.

I am glad you have the opportunity to share your story. We are both being asked to communicate to the public. Not easy, but if we don't respond to this calling, it could be much harder than just allowing it to happen. I feel a deep sense of gratitude. Who would have thought my little studio would be on TV? In some way or another, with the help of God and others, including yourself, I laid the groundwork for that. I say BRAVO for both of us.

Thanks for the chili recipe! I will try it this evening.

Love always, Mom

March 14, 2001

A Letter from Janet's Journal:

Dear God,

    I continue to weed my garden. Clearing my mind of negative thoughts and all that chatter, making room for divine guidance to come through. Springtime arrives next week. I must weed the gardens of my mind, heart, and soul so they will flourish and bear fruit.

    Aliveness returns to me. Once again I hear the birds sing. Again, I feel the sun's penetrating rays. Again, I feel.

    I am grateful. Thank You, God. Life is good. From my vantage point I can see the richness, the goodness, and most assuredly, the oneness with You. If I could only hold onto this place of well-being. *God, please, please guide me.*

March 15, 2001

An Email to Sean from Grammy Vee, 8:47 a.m.

Hey there, Sean Babes! I received your love message. Thanks. I hope you have a Happy St. Patrick's Day. Remember to wear green. I wouldn't want those girls at school pinching you.

I love you, too! Grammy

March 15, 2001

A Note from Janet's Journal:

Returning home, I walked in and hit the play button on my answering machine. I hoped God had left me a message. He didn't call! My mind resembled the churning undercurrents that disrupt the ocean floors. I must believe this makes way for new things to reveal themselves.

In all of this, I must not lose site of my passion. God will provide for me. Please Janet, keep the faith and the trust!

March 16, 2001

A Letter from Vee's Journal:

Dear God,

I have lost my pink pen. I am sure You don't care.

Last night I had a good meditation with You to shrink the lump in my breast. Sometimes it feels bigger at night, probably because of the way I am lying in bed.

I want to work with You as a partner. I want very much to be rid of this condition, but maybe there is a bigger picture. You may have bigger and better plans for me. I need to relax and let the plan unfold. Please guide me in this and help me to realize the truth.

I have never felt so close to You in my life. Maybe there is more for me to learn. This Lenten season gave me a chance to give up my being judgmental, at least verbally. A lot of releasing and being aware remains to be done. I don't need to be critical anymore. For this I am grateful. Thank You, God.

My Sincere Soul.

March 17, 2001

A Note from Janet's Journal:

Happy St. Patrick's Day!

I thank God for yesterday. It was powerful. It was magical, and it was filled with love. What more could anyone want?

March 19, 2001

A Letter from Janet's Journal:

Dear God,

I am stalled at a crossroad. The urge to write calls me in one direction. I started to write *book* at the end of one road and my search for You at the end of another road. But no — both are the same! My faith is rich, strong, unrelenting, and growing with every passing moment. Faith sustains me on every level. Faith guides me to write.

March 20, 2001

A Note from Janet's Journal:

I am incredibly broke and yet wonderfully happy. I express my gratitude. Today is a sacred day. I let go.

March 22, 2001

A Note from Vee's Journal:

Journey into Soul. This title came to me in the night. Suddenly, I knew I was to write a book. It was as though a light went on in my head. It was 3:05 a.m. when my feet hit the floor. After breakfast, I sipped green tea while writing in my journal. My life as story began to unfold. I began with simple little slices of life.

What does a lump in the breast have to do with one's soul? Everything.

In my living room and dining room table cluttered with income tax receipts and forms, I wondered, "Why now, when under the pressure of taxes, would I want to begin writing a book?" So many "*I shoulds*" in the past, but Spirit moved me. Today, as mounds of paper stared up at me, Spirit struck a match and the fire burned.

It started last night while reading "Hawks Cove" by Susan Wilson. She writes with such imagination, and I was inspired. I have always written with straightforward expressions. Could it be that I, too, could put a little spice into each slice of my life? I need to scatter little gems throughout my story.

March 23, 2001

An Email to Sean from Grammy Vee, 4:00 a.m.

Hi, Sean. Grammy hopes to be there for Grand-parent's Day. I am so proud of you and want to meet your teacher and friends. Maybe it will be a sunny day. Remember the rain last year?

How is Grady? Abby loved staying with him. She said, "He is a wonderful old dog". Abby has gone back to New Mexico, and I miss her. She wanted to meet you, but time didn't allow.

I love you a bushel and a peck and a hug around the neck!

Grammy

March 26, 2001

A Letter from Vee's Journal:

Dear God,

I sincerely want to know what Your plans are for me. They are for my own good, I know that. Help me to let go of the negative thoughts and wrong actions. I want miraculous healings, so that my life will be made whole. I want every cell in my body to be healthy, so that I may have a cheerful heart. Please move in and through me, cleansing my body, physically, emotionally, mentally, and spiritually.

Thank You for all of the above. Accept my gratitude for Your nearness. You have created within me a song of happiness. May I let this light shine so that others can see Your good works.

I have never had to exercise such discipline before. There is a purpose, I know. Guide me in each hour to become unstuck in my heart and to release my fixed ideas.

My Soul.

March 27, 2001

A Letter from Vee's Journal:

Dear God,

I am trying to keep a joyful heart as it helps the immune system. Right now the lump seems bigger and harder. My choosing to be joyful sends a message to my whole being. My words and actions sparkle with appreciation for all my blessings.

My goal is to be *in the moment* and not jump ahead to the *future*. When I bask in Your Presence, my concerns melt away. I constantly affirm Your Presence. What joy is in my heart when I leave it with You.

The freshness and beauty of springtime surrounds me. Yesterday, the ocean waves sparkled and splashed against the rocks like giant fountains. I sat with my friend, Margaret Butterworth, and we basked in our good fortune and wealth. I am richly blessed with much good.

Thank You for Your comforting arms.

My Soul.

March 29, 2001

An Email to Janet from Vee, 4:14 a.m.

Greetings! This is a pre-birthday message. Relax in the moment. Breathe. Feel your heart to see if there is joy there. Put on a smile. Dance. Skip rope. Be open. Do a little flirting. Do have fun-fun-fun.

From the one who gave birth. Mom

March 30, 2001

A Letter from Janet's Journal:

Dear Mom,

This morning, I told myself to take another path, perhaps break a few rules - upset the norm!

I didn't write today. Was not sure why. Just meandered around, filling my soul, I guess. This was okay. Louise gave me the most wonderful massage for my birthday. She is a dear to me. I am grateful beyond words.

Another year has gone by. I am grateful you are here. At times, I wasn't certain you would be here again on my birthday. Mom, you are the best gift I have ever received. I also know that in another year, you may have moved on. In my heart, I know you will always be with me.

So Mom, on your advice, I'm on my way to go get wiggy! Ha! Loved your card. On my way to Grappolo's to meet close friends for dinner. Time to celebrate!

And, Sean, I am thankful for you being in my life. I am forever grateful and will love you forever.

Happy Birthday to ME!

Mom, I love you.

March 30, 2001

A Letter from Vee's Journal:

Dear God,

Today I signed a new contract to live another year. I shall see the blue jays building their nests in the rafters above my studio window again next spring.

The feeling of spring delights my senses. Rains have brought many shades of green to the hills that surround my home.

As I walk the path on the ocean bluff, the freshness of the salty air invigorates me. Marveling at the beauty of blue lupine, orange poppies, and purple clover, I decide to sit amongst the magical carpet of wildflowers.

My blessings abound as I open my arms to the abundance of the Universe. Thank You, for Your everlasting support in resolving my day-to-day issues.

Yes, dear God, I want to live another year!

My Sincere Soul.

March 31, 2001

An Email to Janet from Vee, 4:29 a.m.

Subject: The Morning After

Hope you are continuing your birthday celebration.
Forty-six sounds so young to me, but I was there once
a long time ago. Life brings fascinating changes.
Through them all, we must touch into the present.

Anxious to hear about your dinner last night.
Love, Mom

April 1, 2001

A Letter from Vee's Journal:

Dear God,

I feel lost. My situation consumes my
thoughts. In my meditations, I visualize a stream of
purple light at the crown of my head. It pours down
through me and all around me. At that moment, I
feel Your Presence and realize pure love. Love is the
only thing. I inhale Your perfection and feel it
throughout my body.

Why then, Dear God, do I allow fearful
thoughts to glide into my psyche and gain so much

attention? I seek help from the Divine, and within moments, look to find someone who can help me.

We are partners in this, God, but letting go and leaving my concerns with You, is at times, a struggle.

Bless me as I walk this path, and thank You for holding my hand.

My Heart and Mind,

May they both open fully.

April 2, 2001

A Letter from Vee's Journal:

Dear God,

I feel a definite shift in my relationship with You, a sort of melting down, letting go, letting You.

It started at church yesterday when the gathering focused on healing. Circled in chairs with John Allan as the facilitator, we took turns sharing anything that bubbled up. There was talk of asking for help. I have never been very good at asking as I always think I must do it myself. Well, I am asking for help now. I need Your help!

You have been watching over me, but now I am letting you make the decisions. I am in Your hands. I will respond and take action. Just let me know what to do.

I am willing to change.

My Heart, Soul, and Mind.

April 3, 2001
A Note from Vee's Journal:

Another week passed without much writing. Maybe just writing in my journals was capturing a slice of life.

Judith gave me a healing session with both of us totally open to whatever would happen. I felt grounded when it was over. My body felt like wood. Perhaps that was what I needed because my thoughts were spinning off in every direction, and I doubted my decisions. Leaving it with God was the right thing to do.

Such a bumpy road - this path. The main thing is to not get stuck in a rut. Be open - and if I start to close down - catch it. Open. Turn it around.

Everyday I give thanks for the people in my life.

I sense a shift. I feel a turning point. I will pray.

April 20, 2001

A Letter from Vee's Journal:

Dear God,

Last night the lump in my breast was acting up. I slept well, but off and on. During the night, I affirmed Your Presence and Your healing currents of love. I tried to figure out what to do. Do I use my arm too much? Help me to know. Reveal to me the causes, and I will gladly eliminate them from my life. I want only to serve You. Perhaps I should express more of Your bounteous works to my clients and friends.

Be with me as I go to a retreat at Zaca Lake for three days. I am not afraid. With Your love and healing power, I will continue to go. Let my light so shine that I will be a blessing to others.

My Heart, Soul, and Mind.

April 26, 2001

A Letter from Vee's Journal:

Dear God,

Thank You for my many blessings. First of all, the retreat at Zaca Lake, the special belonging that I felt with the people there, the peppering of snow on Saturday morning, the calmness of the lake on Sunday morning creating a peaceful atmosphere.

Even the rare head cold I had was a blessing. It was time to rest and release, knowing that there is Divine order in Your plan. I gave up control and decided to be with *what is*. I have had good practice with that, but it seems that I need a little more.

I am grateful to the Reiki Master who willingly initiated me into Reiki II and III. I can now teach

Reiki. It is my passion to help people to heal each other or to assist in their own healing. My prayers have been answered.

May I use this new venture to the best of my ability and for Your glory. There is a sudden shift, could this be an answer to a prayer?

My Heart, Mind, Soul.

April 28, 2001

A Letter from Vee's Journal:

Dear God,

I have this deep longing to know what is right for me. Sometimes the path seems clear and at other times uncertain. All I really need to know is that You are always working with me. The decisions are mine to make, but You have the blueprint to my soul. I want to know when it is time to turn a corner or go straight. Guide me, be with me, and enfold me in Your love, peace, and harmony.

Help me to trust. Help me to look openly at my shadow side. Shed Your light on any darkness.

Thank You for all of the above. It is done. I am filled with compassion for all beings everywhere.

From within my deepest Self.

May 1, 2001

An Email to Janet from Vee, 7:14 a.m.

Such a beautiful day! I want to share my happiness with you. Just finished a meditation. My friend gave me two tapes by Tara Brach, a Buddhist Nun, on Radical Self-Acceptance. They are great and just what I have been doing in my emotional release with others. Today, I worked on myself. I felt the trauma in my throat. All the time I thought it was my breast. Interesting. We always have work to do. What a relief to shake it off.

McCall sounds like a wonderful plan. It will be good to see all of my children at one time.

The workshop at the Episcopal Church is July 20-21, and I have committed myself to do healing work there. We had a meeting yesterday, and it is being well planned and sounds like fun. Maybe you can come.

I am off for my morning walk.

Toodles. Mom

May 2, 2001

A Letter from Janet's Journal:

Dear Mom,

Intense sadness engulfs me. I cannot shake my thoughts that one day you will be moving on. I long to feel an intense joy-- the same joy I experienced with Grandpa Mauk. On one level, I try. Like I said to Sean last night, "I can't imagine my mom not being here." I reach to find the joy and instead cry out, "I am not ready for this!"

All of yesterday I kept diverting my attention to McCall. I was on the phone trying to work out a reservation for the Armstrong Cabin. I want to take Sean there. I want to take Jessa there. As I am about to confirm a week in August, you phone with the news of your breast mass. As I carefully listened to your plans for seeing a physician, part of me wanted to run. Fast and far away. The other part of me is determined to stay, to continue walking the road with you.

During our phone conversation I heard you asking for prayers and I became very attentive. I even grabbed a pen. I wanted to write *your* prayer down just as *you* wish. It would have been easier to change the prayer and make it my prayer. You said to me that you had no regrets and that you wished to be guided to do the right thing. I knew the truth and the possibilities that could come from this. To surrender completely without attaching an outcome, and to be open to the Will of God, not yours. Powerful! You are brave and courageous. I wish this for myself.

I am torn. Your prayer is to follow God's plan. My prayer is for you not to die.

We fight to hang on to our loved ones, and in doing so, interfere in their processes. I don't wish to interfere with yours, Mom. I love you very much, and my wish is not to hold you back in any way. I pray for God to help me with this. I feel as though I have just detached a bit from it all. So for now,

I offer a prayer,

Dear God,

Please guide me daily to continue in my soul work in search for Truth and to do Your Will. Guide me to be aware and to follow my intuition. Make me a servant to Your needs. I ask that the Holy Spirit fill my being and replace my thoughts of fear with thoughts of Love. I ask that I find a way in my heart to accept that which is. Teach me to love and to be loved. Teach me to fear not this Love for it is Your Love. May I be open to Divine timing with all my vacation plans, whether or not we go to McCall or somewhere else. Teach me to learn about money, how to handle it, and how not to be attached to it. May it never again dictate whether or not I have joy in my life. I ask that I live today fully in the moment with the Christ mind and Buddha's compassionate heart. May I spread this out wherever I go, knowing I am safe wherever I am and am safe wherever I go. And again, I will pray for my mom.

Sending you love, Mom.
And so it is.

May 4, 2001

A Letter from Vee's Journal:

Dear God,

Please help me to be open to whatever is for my highest good. Free me from limitations and judgments. Open to any possibility. The choices are mine to make, but I seek answers from You.

If fear creeps in, cast it out, but only after it has been experienced and felt. Thank You for expressing Yourself through my body and mind. May Your light shine through my soul.

I am expressing victory over each and every difficulty. Thanks be. May I embrace the shadow deities of my Self. Always learning.

A Thankful Heart.

May 6, 2001

A Letter from Janet's Journal:

Dear Mom,

Just discussed the McCall trip with Jessa. The conversation went from McCall to you and your impending doctor's appointment. Ten days away on May 16, 2001 at 10:30 a.m., you will know the answer to the question that has remained unanswered now for more than two years.

Nausea overtakes me. Jessa leaves, and I feel more of it. Who will be with you when you go to the appointment? Who will be with you afterwards? Who will be with you when you need them? Will you ask for help when you need it? Please do! I will send you a note card tomorrow to please ask me when you need me. I am here for you, Mom. My schedule does not matter. All will work out according to Divine order. I am grateful for whatever happens, and I thank God. May I continue to express my gratitude.

Instead of saying, "I can't imagine life without you," I change my thought pattern. My affirmation for today is, "May your Spirit shine through wherever you are." May I remain open to the experience always.

I offer a prayer,

Please, Dear God, may my mother be guided to make the right decision by Divine order. May Your will, not that of mine and others, but Your will be done. Thank you very much. Love You with all my heart and soul. And so it is.

May 6, 2001

A Letter from Vee's Journal:

Dear God,

The moon was beautiful last night glowing through the pines. Almost full. I believe it will be full tonight. Today the sun is shining and warm. Thank You for Your marvelous works in nature.

I feel certain that my choice to see a surgeon is valid. It is my opening to the Divine within the medical field. Warped by my limited thinking due to what I had seen in the past, I let go of that belief system knowing that You are in the hospitals, too. I will take You with me, and as the story unfolds, see God in the eyes of everyone and every situation. May others see God in my eyes.

Be with me today and everyday.

My Soul.

May 8, 2001 6:11 a.m.

An Email to Janet from Vee:

Jessa offered to come up and drive me to Templeton. I had already made plans with Judith, but I thought it was so sweet of Jessa to want to do it. I have a good support system here. It is always good to have family, though. You have done plenty for me. I am actually looking forward to my visit. It is time. I had to go all the way down deep before I could emerge again.

The moon was beautiful here, too. Especially this morning. I went out on my deck before daylight. The weather has been warm for Cambria.

Toodles, Mom

May 10, 2001

A Letter from Vee's Journal:

Dear God,

     I feel that there is some kind of resolving going on with my breast issue. My attitude has changed and a dream I had the other night makes me feel everything is going to be all right.

<u>The Dream:</u> A gigantic horse came along while I was sitting at the beach. It was walking by the waterfront. It looked ferocious! It circled around and came towards me at a fast pace. Scary! Then, with a change of pace, it circled around behind me and barely brushed the back of my head. It felt more like a comforting caress.

I believe the dragon and demons are being removed from my body. Only sweet music now.

Thank You for Your perfect unfoldment.

My Soul.

May 13, 2001, *Mother's Day*

A Letter from Janet's Journal:

Dear Mom,

I sit here in my orange chair feeling gratitude along with despair. My gratitude is felt for the experience of having shared a wondrous Mother's Day with you yesterday. The despair stems from my own inability to face my own mortality.

You are going in on Wednesday to have your breast examined and will be contemplating surgery at that time. You are facing the truth of what has been in your breast for almost two years. I struggle. I am human. I am your daughter. You are my mother. And while I support you and your every decision, I cannot and will not deny my own sadness or my own pain.

How does one prepare for this? It is part of your journey. It also is part of my journey.

I ask God for strength and courage. I ask God to grant you the strength, courage, and wisdom to guide you. May God's love and light fill you. May the Holy Spirit continue to guide us. I love you.

May 13, 2001

A Letter from Vee's Journal:

Dear God,

A real concern. The mirror on the shower door revealed the truth. It was discouraging to see the lump in my breast growing and changing color. For many months it had remained the same size. Please help me! I am afraid.

May 14, 2001

A Letter from Vee's Journal:

Dear God,

I am back in the pink again, with my pen at least. For several days the pen had been missing. Writing with a pink pen warms my heart. Pink reminds me of Love.

I am working on the part of myself that seems out of balance. Cleaning my stove the other day threw me into a negative state. I didn't know I was hurting myself until that night. The breast tissue was complaining. It had been sensitive for about three days now. I was doing so well. More learning for me to do I guess.

My affirmation is: *I accept my God given perfection. I realize I need a shift in my thinking. Please grant this perfection and thank You in advance.*

My Self.

I honestly believe that everything happens for my highest good. My question is: *How can anything good come out of this predicament?*

The good? It forced me into a crisis. I knew I needed help. I had run into a wall. On the phone with my acupuncturist, I explained my situation. I was impressed with her knowledge of words. She lived close by. I explained my situation. "Do you think you could help?" I said desperately, clinging to the phone.

"I wouldn't feel comfortable working without more information. There is a wonderful surgeon over in Templeton by the name of Michelle Strasen."

The minute she mentioned the name, I knew surgery was my only option. It was the same surgeon Dr. Wilson had recommended on my first exam. When you hear a name twice, it rings a bell. The bell that went off was *YES!*

May 15, 2001

A Letter from Vee's Journal:

Dear God,

Tomorrow I will see the surgeon. May I seek Your Presence all day long. The time has arrived and I ask to be divinely guided. If there has been any lack in the unfoldment of this situation, please reveal it to me so that I might learn. I'll have to admit, I feel kind of shaky about it, even though it seems right. It is throwing me into unfamiliar territory.

I am asking for Your divine guidance. Help me to remember that I still have choices. Thank You for all the people who are supporting me. I appreciate them.

My Sincere Self.

P. S. I need to be open to who I <u>really</u> am!

I have just received a note card from Janet. It reads:

May 17, 2001

Dear Mom,

    I will keep you in my thoughts and prayers. I know you will be guided to do the right thing. I pray that you be given courage, strength, and wisdom at this time on your journey. I am grateful Judith will be taking you.

    May God be with you and bless you.

    I love you, Janet

P.S. I've enclosed a special prayer for Wednesday morning and the little bouquet is to lay on your pillow while you sleep.

~ 11 ~

THE NEWS

May 17, 2001

A Note from Vee's Journal:

A moment ago, a bird knocked on the back of my house. I assume it was a bird. I ask, *What is the message? What do you want to say to me?* With my left hand I write:

Just have hope. Know it will be all right. Stop, look and listen.

Show the world who you really are, a child of God here to express joy and love.

A Note from Vee's Journal, *evening entry*:

Tonight, I reflect on the day's events. Judith had driven me to the surgeon's office in Templeton. As we walked into the reception area, I glanced around the room. The wallpaper on the wall, the early American furniture, and the choice of magazines made me feel at home. It could have been anyone's living room. I felt a closeness to the surgeon even before I met her.

The receptionist handed me the usual forms. This feels right, I thought as the questionnaire was completed. After handing the papers back to the receptionist, I joined Judith, and we discussed Larry Dossey's book, *Reinventing Medicine.* It had sparked something within me a few months before, and it was important to share it with others.

A nurse appeared and motioned for me to come with her. "It's all right for you to come too," she announced to Judith. As Judith and I walked side-by-side down the hall our connection deepened. Together we passed through the doorway.

"Do you want me to be with you?" Judith turned to ask me.

"My feeling is that I would like to be alone," I said, knowing she would understand.

"That was my feeling," she said as she left the room.

The nurse handing me the pink gown said, "This is one-size-fits-all!" It was the prettiest paper gown I had ever seen, but you could have wrapped it around me three times. I sat alone staring at the walls and cabinets.

The door opened. In walked Dr. Michelle Strasen. Somehow I thought of Shelly Winters. She stood tall, blond, full-breasted, and wearing a casual dress. She graciously shook my hand, sat down on a rolling stool before me, and looked up into my eyes.

"What can I do for you?"

Somehow my story of the past year and nine months was revealed in one minute. My search to know myself. She looked somewhat puzzled, but proceeded with the examination. After checking my right breast, she sat down on her rolling stool again.

"Just how aggressive do you want me to be?" she asked.

"I want to know what you are thinking," I bravely answered.

"I am almost certain it is cancer."

It came as no shock. We discussed the options of having a biopsy before or at the time of surgery. Then it became very clear to me and I said, "I feel that sometimes a biopsy can spread the disease. It is my choice to wait until the day of surgery."

She left the exam room while I dressed. My mind raced back and forth concerning the biopsy. Maybe I had read too many books or my feelings were still fighting the medical profession.

Approaching the receptionist, I noticed Dr. Strasen bending over the counter in a huddle with her staff. She was discussing the scheduling of my upcoming surgery. I approached her and interrupted with my need to learn and understand. "Excuse me. I need to talk to you more about the biopsy."

Dr. Strasen immediately escorts me back to the examining room. I explained my feelings again while she pulled the metal cart up close. As I watch her reach for what looked like the needle used for biopsies, it suddenly did not feel right to me. "I think I'll wait."

Respecting my decision, she begins to place the instruments back in the cabinet. We both exit the exam room once again together.

"How soon can we do the surgery?"

"Within a week," she assured me.

Relieved over my decision, I left with the necessary forms in hand for my pre-op tests. Somewhat in a daze, I walked out of the building to find Judith sitting on a bench outside the door. It was a pleasant day. The sun was shining and the bench felt warm. Sitting there together I repeated the doctor's words, *the almost certainty that it was cancer.*

As we sat quietly for a few minutes, I greatly appreciated Judith's loving energy. Her presence comforted me beyond words. Suddenly the realization of the financial part hit me.

"I do not know how much all of this will cost."

"That has nothing to do with it," Judith assured me.

"You are right, of course. Let's go have the tests."

I saw no reason to delay once it was apparent that surgery was my course of action. Back in the car, we drove two blocks to Twin Cities Hospital.

After lunch there in the cafeteria, we spent the afternoon moving from one lab to another. I felt grateful to have Judith as my friend and guide. The procedures were new to me, since I had not done anything like this for twenty-two years. The *what if's* crept in and made me feel uneasy. I wondered as the nurse drew blood if it were the right color. *Was mine different?* It looked purple. The nurse assured me it was a normal color.

Next we found our way down the hall for an EKG. I would have much preferred a KEG. I couldn't believe the speed of the EKG machine. Things had certainly changed.

With the tests behind me, we drove toward Cambria allowing ourselves time to soak in the beauty of Highway 46 surrounded by the vibrant rows of vineyards dispersed among the rolling hills. Inhaling the freshness of the air after the recent rains, we quietly made our way home.

A Letter from Vee's Journal, *evening entry*:
Dear God,

The news from the surgeon is that the lump in my breast is most likely cancer. It came as no shock, as I was willing to face that reality in September of 1999. Knowing that possibility, it was still necessary for me to go deep within my soul and search for the reason.

I believe the time spent on this journey has not been in vain. So much joy and bliss have come my way. My spiritual community is vitally important to me. I have had to awaken to the areas within me where I must grow.

Now, with Your help, I will focus on getting rid of the tumor and releasing the dark cells that have invaded my body.

My Self.

May 18, 2001

A Letter from Vee's Journal:

Dear God,

Let me feel Your presence in every cell of my body, cleansing and purifying, making me whole.

Be with me throughout the day. Your strength will supply my every need.

I must learn to allow others to help me. Surrendering all to You.

When Dr. Strasen calls today with a date for surgery may we combine our energies with Yours and be Divinely guided.

The unknown is scary. You are my Shepherd, a very present help in time of trouble.

Thank You for this day, and all the blessings that go with it!

My Self.

May 18, 2001

A Note from Vee's Journal:

I am still waiting to hear from Dr. Strasen about the lab reports. She will call me when she receives the results, and we will set a date for surgery.

The greatest lesson for me at this time is to release old, fixed beliefs and ideas, which include doctors and hospitals. This is what the lymph system is all about. I want to know who I am. When I rid myself of the garbage, I will become clear and be able to see the real me. I must ride on the waves of the unknown and dance with life.

About fear? When it rears its ugly face, I visualize that face turning into many smiley faces. Dancing.

~ 12 ~

SUPPORT TEAM

May 19, 2001 8:07

An Email to Janet from Vee:

<u>Subject</u>: On friendship by George Elliott

"Oh, the comfort, the inexpressible comfort of feeling safe with a person; having neither to weigh thoughts nor measure words, but to pour them all out just as they are, chaff and grain together, knowing that a faithful hand will take and sift them, keeping what is worth keeping, and, then, with a breath of kindness, blow the rest away."

Thank you for being my friend, Janet.

Toodles, Mom

May 19, 2001

A Letter from Vee's Journal:

Dear God,

I allowed fear to enter my body yesterday. It seems that when I tell certain people about my condition, it creates worry on their part. This is why I didn't want to tell people at the beginning of my journey. The beautiful souls at Unity Church and my family have been lovingly supportive. Their prayers have sustained me. I'm happy to have shared my journey with these positive people.

I have meditated, prayed, and had a positive outlook. Yet, with all of this, the lump remains. Help me! Remove the fear. I accept complete responsibility for the situation. Help me to relax with the uncertainty.

There is only one alternative to fear, and that is trust. I trust. I trust. I trust.

Shed Your light upon me. Renew my spirit. May I feel Your loving embrace.

My Self.

May 20, 2001

A Letter from Janet's Journal:

Dear Mom,

Thank you for your email last night. I felt warmed to hear that I am your friend. You, too, are my friend.

This past week you told me you will have surgery. They will be removing your breast. I will be there for you, now more than ever.

Mom, I love you!

<u>My dream on awakening this morning:</u> I walk up beside my friend, Laura Wilkening, and say, "She (my mom) is getting ready to go." Laura warmly replies, "Oh, I'm so glad. She'll be fine."

For now, I offer a prayer,

Dear God,

Please guide me today. I open myself to the Holy Spirit, and may the Holy Spirit fill my mind, and my body. May I be courageous when I need the courage, and may I break down when I need to break down. I don't want to go to that place of fear. Please help me. I pray for my mom. May she be filled with Your love and light.

Amen.

May 22, 2001

An Email to Sean from Grammy:

Dear Sean, I know how much you are missing your dog, Grady. I am praying that God will enfold you in His arms and comfort you just as He does me. I am glad you have friends. They help when you are sad. Grady is no longer hurting. He is in a joyous place. Trust that.

I will be seeing you soon. My surgery is scheduled for Friday.

I love you more than you love me!!!!! So there!

Grammy

May 22, 2001

Sean writes out a prayer for the prayer group at Unity Church in Cambria. It reads:

> To the grammy becaus she has surgry on her brest becouse of a lump She can't and she can't dri ve musagh

May 23, 2001

A Note from Janet's Journal:

Sitting here with a head full of acupuncture needles, I journal. It's a tough day as I think about leaving town tomorrow to be with my mom. I feel overwhelmed and scared about her undergoing surgery. My thoughts jump to the idea of painting her toenails. She has decided on mauve. She shaved her legs for the occasion and wants to make her toes pretty. I love it.

A needle falls out of my ear. I hand it to Sean who places it carefully back in it's casing and then pretends he is going to shoot it at me. He brings it to his mouth, points it at me and says, "Heads up!" Now what is a nervous mother to do? I can't help but smile. I love him next to me. He keeps pretending he is going to shoot me. The sound effects are tremendous. He brings me joy.

I leave the acupuncturist, feeling much calmer.

~ 13 ~

SURRENDERING

May 24, 2001

On the eve of surgery, Sean and I arrive at my mom's. We greet briefly and then begin our dance of avoidance. As she moves across the living room, I watch her, study her. Is she frightened? I am terrified. Is she worried? I am panicked. Is she peaceful? My guts are churning. She moves toward a drawer and opens it.

"This is where I keep my checkbook. The bills here are not due to be paid yet. I will take care of them when I return. I also have a little bit of cash."

I look and listen but from a distance. I don't want to know this information. I don't want to deal with any of it should the need arise. I fear it will. For the first time, I realize that I can't even speak. My gut tightens, and I rush to the bathroom. I want to throw up, but I can't. I have to be here for her.

God, please help me.

I think about how Lissa has volunteered to help. Bless her. I am relieved, even though I'm not sure how I will need her. The pressure is off just in knowing that she could, and would, drive my mother to the hospital first thing in the morning. My mind races back to fear.

God, if I am this sick now, what will I be like in the morning? Please fill me with Your love and light.

Right now she is in bed writing a letter to God. I wonder what she is saying. I have a few things myself to say to God right now. Right now, I don't believe the old saying, "We are never given more than we can handle." Bullshit!

I have so many questions and time is running out. I do know that she couldn't breast feed Karen and me because we were in the incubator. I'm mourning the loss of her breast. Tomorrow, they will cut into her body, into her breast. Intense grief blasts me without warning, and I am confused at the depths of my feelings, my sadness, and my grief.

God, I don't want to be sick tomorrow. I want to be there for her all the way. And I want to be strong.

I continue to sit in the chair that I think belonged to my grandmother. I don't know for sure. I will ask Mom tomorrow. Glancing around the walls, my gaze stops on every one of her paintings. I want to buy one. It will be mine. Tomorrow I will ask my mom which one she wants me to have. The questions are irrelevant. The real issue is that I'm not finished with her being my mom. I 'm not ready to let go.

Thoughts of her dying in surgery race through my mind and fear pummels my body. Is this normal? There is risk with general anesthesia. What will happen?

God, I hate this! Every bit of it! It isn't fair! You know the outcome already. In the meantime, I have to live on the edge. My fear consumes me.

Please, help me. Teach me, God. I am open and willing. I am listening.

Calmness filters through me. As I make up my bed, I sort through her bedding and massage sheets. I can smell her on them, a combination of the massage oils she uses. I want to lie in these sheets and blankets and allow the scents to envelop me — to calm me on every level. Sean snuggles in close. I wrap my arm around him.

"Mama? If Grammy dies, do we get her paintings?"

"Oh, I don't know," I respond lovingly. I don't want to go there. My mind wanders to the things in her home, her artifacts and treasures. I wish I knew more about them. I see the shepherd in the window and remembered when she carved it. Her creativity and talent are awe-inspiring. She succeeds in everything she tries.

I crave a glass of wine, but a part of me says no. I cannot numb myself in any way. My mom may die, and I must be there for her.

"Bless you, Mom. I love you. It's okay for you to cry, Mom. Thank You, God, for I am grateful to be here with her, grateful that we have this time together," I say quietly and drift into a deep sleep.

May 24, 2001, *evening time*
A Letter from Vee's Journal:
Dear God,

We have come to the night before surgery. Thank You for the people in my life. So much love. Be with me and everyone involved as we move through the day tomorrow. Fill our hearts with peace. Let us feel Your Presence, strength, and comfort. Enfold us in Your mighty arms.

> *The Lord is my shepherd. I shall*
> *not want.*
> *He maketh me to lie down in green*
> *pastures. He restoreth*
> *my soul. Yeah, though I walk*
> *through the valley of the*
> *shadow of death, I will fear no evil.*
> *Thy rod and thy staff,*
> *they comfort me.*

I leave it all to You, God, and I know You are with me through each moment.

My Self.

~ 14 ~

UNWAVERING FAITH

May 25, 2001, *The Day of Surgery*

VEE   I watched daylight emerge through the
skylight in my bedroom. The comforter on my four-
poster bed felt cozy and warm. A slight breeze
blowing through the window just above my head
carried fresh air to bring me to a fully awakened state.

That was when I remembered the plans for the day. Surgery!

I thought about Janet and Sean sleeping downstairs. They would be eating breakfast, but since there was to be no food or water after midnight for me, I decided to stay out of the kitchen. There would be no long walk through the woods either. Might as well shower and pack my over-nighter. I felt calm and peaceful as my feet touched the floor. As I switched on my bedroom lamp, I noticed the figure of Kuan Yin sitting under the fringe of my peach colored lampshade. Janet had given me this angel of Mercy on my birthday. My house is full of thoughtful cards and treasures from this endearing child. She will be there to comfort me today.

JANET   I awaken to noise in the living room. "Mom, is that you?"

"Yes."

"How are you feeling?"

"I'm okay, just getting my things ready."

I wake Sean up by kissing my favorite place on his forehead and whisper, "We need to get up and take Grammy to the hospital, Sweetie."

VEE   We were to leave the house at 7:00 a.m. My friend, Lissa, arrived on my doorstep right on time with a gift from my daughter, Karen. She was unable to be with me today. A large basket of natural wood filled with lotions, candles, and soaps. The Lavender scent permeated the room. We would carry a fresh sprig of Rosemary to the hospital with us. Rosemary is for remembrance. I thought of those who were with me in spirit, especially my daughter, Jessa.

As we walked through the ivy-covered arbor on the way to the car, Lissa pulled some polished rocks from a bag and said, "Take one." The gold letters on mine read TRUST. That I did.

JANET   Wow! What a nice gift from Karen. I wonder if she wishes she were here. Outside the four of us stand in a circle. Holding hands, I try desperately to breath. Lissa has us each take a rock from a velvet bag. Sean chooses COURAGE, Grammy, TRUST, Lissa LOVE, and mine HEALING. We walk to our cars quietly. Lissa pulls out in front of me and drives slowly down the road. Taking hold of my rock I pray for courage and strength. Will my mom return here? I pull out to follow and hear Sean's heavy sigh.

"You okay, Mom?"

"Yeah," quietly looking in his direction. What a sensitive gem of a son I have.

VEE I decided to ride with Lissa since she was alone. Janet and Sean followed in their van. Rounding a curve we spotted a deer, a sign of gentleness. I was embracing the dark in order to find the light. The deer for me meant safety in my journey. A feeling of protection washed over me.

"Lissa," I said, "this is such delightful country. I chose Twin Cities Hospital because it is surrounded by beauty."

"You're right. If you look in the field on your left, you will see a small rabbit."

"Isn't it amazing that all the animals are appearing to say hello and embrace us on our way," I remarked. I was hoping Janet and Sean had seen the rabbit, too. I look back at her van following us.

"Janet is right on our bumper. I know she needs to be close."

"I was noticing and thinking the same thing," said Lissa, smiling.

Green trees mean healing to me. At one time, a canopy of green graced us as it arched over the road. These Coastal Oaks caught my breath as we drove through. An inspirational moment.

JANET   I notice a deer off in the woods and smile. Then I focus on Lissa's car ahead of me. I can see the silhouette of my mom's head through the window. I am quiet. I am peaceful. I cling to the energy field of Lissa and my mom and can't help but drive too close behind. *Am I tailgating her?* Yes. I back away, but this feels distressing. I pull in closer. I need to be close! I need to be there for her! I'm here for you, Mom. I'm right here!

We turn onto a magically beautiful road completely enveloped by trees stretching out to provide a canopy. As we make our way through the curves, I feel protected and peaceful even during this time of uncertainty. I don't know where the road leads except we are all on the way to the hospital.

VEE   As we entered the hospital parking lot, I pointed, "Look at those two spaces just waiting for us."

Lissa parked her car, and Janet pulled in beside us. Strolling into the hospital, we let our presence be known to the pink ladies at the front desk. Sean, still sleepy, took over a big couch in the lobby with doggie, a favorite stuffed animal curled under his arm.

"Here, Grammy, take Doggie for good luck."

An attractive, up-beat nurse appeared and called out my name. I joined her, and as she led me down the hall, my heart began to pound. A moment of fright. I didn't speak. This surprised me, as I had felt so calm. By the time the nurses had placed all my belongings in their proper places, the panic had left. Once again, solitude comforted me.

JANET   Once there, we sit together in the waiting room. A nurse calls for my mom. Sean curls up on the couch with blanket and pillow. I get some paper from one of the volunteers. She motions to Sean, "Is the young boy sick?"

"No, his Grammy is having surgery today." She nods.

A nurse takes Mom and we wait. Later she takes us to her. The hallway is filled with the familiar smell of a hospital cafeteria. Thank goodness I'm not hungry. Entering her room, we find her propped up, her arms wrapped around Sean's doggie. She looks like a precious child. I smile and she smiles back, but no one speaks.

Lissa takes Lavender oil from her bag and begins to anoint my mom. Scent fills the room. I take in a deep breath and reach for her feet. Holding them, I send my love through touch. Then I begin to massage. I don't want this to end. Two hours until surgery. I need more time. *Two hours is not enough time, God.*

VEE   My dear friend Jane arrived and applied the ancient healing system of Reiki to my right side. Lissa directed healing energy on my left side. Janet lovingly massaged and held my feet. She had polished my toenails red the night before. With a little glitter sprinkled on the tops, I was assured the most beautiful feet to have ever entered those surgery doors. My grandson, Sean, was a pure delight while everyone was soothing me with their loving touches. He will never know how much his presence meant to me. He was hungry upon arrival to the hospital, and it didn't take him long to find food. A drink with a straw eighteen inches long and a sweet treat brought happiness to his dear soul. When the surgeon visited our room she asked, "Sean, do you have any questions?"

"Yes. Is this a donut?"

"No, I think that's a Honey-bun," she answered. Surgeons need to know a lot!

Suddenly Sean was out the door once again and reappeared promptly with a small vase of flowers, a mixed bouquet. Placing the vase upon my stomach he says, "They cost nine dollars and fifty cents exactly." He was a good shopper. He explained to me that there was another vase there, but "It only had two little old daisies in it."

"Oh, Sean, thanks. I love you," I smiled.

"I love YOU more than you love me!"

"No, I love YOU more than you love me!"

Out the door once more, back in a few minutes with a colorful drawing he had prepared for me. It was made up of bright wavy lines. Jane exclaimed,

"I'm afraid you are going to short out the equipment in the Operating Room!"

Everyone laughed, even Janet.

JANET   Sean breaks the silence and announces that he's going for hot chocolate. I am relieved that he knows his way around and appreciate that I can stay here. Jane Wheeler walks in. We've spoken only on the phone. It is nice to put a face with the voice. She takes my mom's hand and gently places her other hand on my mom's shoulder, takes a deep breath, and closes her eyes. We are my mom's disciples, all fully present in the moment, nurturing and loving her tenderly. I am surprised that I have maintained a sense of calm. Sean returns to the room, happy and content, holding a cup of hot chocolate and a large cinnamon roll. He takes one look at us, puts his things down, and comes to the foot of the bed. He puts a hand up on his Grammy's leg. He is part of this.

VEE   I had planned to say a prayer. The surgeon was most willing to join us. She laid her right hand on my shoulder and took Janet's hand with her left. I had chosen a prayer from Marianne Williamson's book, *"Illuminata"*. Everyone joined hands while I read.

JANET   Nurses are coming and going, and suddenly I become aware of a change. The energy field in the room is shifting. Not only my mom and the four of us, but the nurses who were once bustling in and out are now moving slowly, calmly.

"What is that wonderful fragrance?" one of them asked.

"Lavender."

We quiet our minds and continue our work, which spreads out into the room and spills into the hallway. My mom wanted it to spill into the operating room and surround all who were involved.

Dr. Strasen enters, introduces herself to everyone, and joins us in prayer. We gather around the gurney. My mom, holding Marianne Williamson's "*Illuminata*," begins to read, 'Gratitude for the Body'. Dr. Strasen holds my hand firmly, and as my mom reads on, caresses the top of my hand with hers. I am comforted. She is with me in every way. I listen as my mom reads.

VEE   *Dear God,*
          As I rise up, I thank You for the
opportunity to be on this earth.
          I thank You for my mind and body.
          I thank You for my life.
          Please bless my body and use it for Your
purposes.
          May I rise up strong today, and may my
body and soul radiate Your love.
          May all impurities be cast out of my
mind, my heart, my body.
          May every cell of my being be filled with
Your light.   ·
          May my body and mind both be
illumined for Your sake and for the sake of all the world.
Amen.

A nurse came in and Janet asked how long until they would be taking me in for surgery.

"I'd say in about two hours," she replied.

It was approaching noon, and I suggested that everyone grab a bite to eat. They agreed.

I lay there, but I was not alone. The love and support filtered through every fiber of my being. In no time at all, a tall man stood at the head of my bed, clipboard in hand, taking notes.

"Are you allergic to any medications?"

"Not to my knowledge. Are you the anesthesiologist?"

"Yes."

"Are you taking me to surgery *now*?" I noticed a nurse at his side.

"Yes," they answered in unison.

I became highly excited, because Janet and my group had been waiting so faithfully all morning to be with me, and I had sent them away for lunch.

"But you have to wait! Janet isn't here! They're in the cafeteria!" I yelled.

Sensing my alarm, the nurse said, "I'll get her. What is she wearing?"

"A lavender sweater!"

Within moments Janet flew into the room with Sean trailing on her heels. The nurse popped a blue surgery cap on my head as they quickly moved the gurney into the hall.

"Oh, the cap matches my gown. How lovely!" I said, but no one seemed to hear me. Janet walked silently beside my gurney.

JANET   The four of us leave to grab a bite to eat and walk slowly toward the cafeteria. We eat outside at a picnic table.

"Can I give you a Reiki treatment, Janet?" Jane asks.

"Oh, yes, I would love it!" I said, wanting to divert my attention. Just as Jane is about to begin, a scrub nurse approaches.

"We are taking Velma in for surgery now."

Down the hall I race. As I arrive at her room, people are moving her out. I approach the side of her gurney and frantically place my hand on it. There she is, smiling, of course. I look at her, and my mind begs. *Please, God, keep her safe. Please don't take her now. Please.*

I say nothing as I grasp the side rails as though clutching her life. The large metal doors marked Operating Room swing open. I lean over and kiss her cheek. My tears form quickly as I whisper, "I love you, Mom."

"I'll be fine," she says and smiles warmly.

I stand staring at the closed doors, alone in my thoughts and completely unaware of Sean, Lissa, and Jane at my side.

"Oh, she'll be just fine." I look up to see a nurse smiling. She is trying to comfort me, but her statement sounds shallow. How does she know?

I consciously make a choice not to jump into fear and doubt, two weapons I had armed myself with in the past. They no longer serve me. Walking away, I say silently, *"I pray you are okay, Mom."*

VEE   An all-encompassing peace prevailed as they rolled me from my room to surgery. Total surrender to the NOW. Although someone was playing a song by Willie Nelson on the speaker system, and even though I was not comfortable with Willie Nelson, I held my peace in connection with God. God and I were One. Judith had arranged for several people to gather in her home to meditate while the surgery was being performed. I could feel the joining of energies. Without fear, I took a deep breath. That was the last thing I remembered.

JANET   After a thirty-minute break outside by a noisy generator, we come back in. Sean walks beside me, oblivious to everything until he spots a door with a long narrow window and peers in.

      "What is that man doing, Mama?"

      My only clue is the sign on the door. Pathologist. I take a peek. A man is seated at his desk peering into a microscope. It hits me. Is he examining the breast tissue from my mom's biopsy? This is all too real. Earlier I had seen the Admission Slip: Right Breast Biopsy with Probable Right Breast Mastectomy. I want to yell through the small window, "Is it malignant or is it benign?" I wanted to know now!

My thoughts jump back to my mom. Why? Why her? For someone who had worked so hard healing others and most courageously looked upon this mass as a teacher of compassion and love, to be losing a breast is undeserving. Why does this have to be?

I join Sean and Lissa, and we find a tree on a small patch of lawn just outside the entrance. We nestle into the coolness of the damp grass. I watch as Sean climbs the tree.

"Here give me your foot." I lie back, and as Lissa begins applying cool lotion and massaging my foot, I realize I am in heaven. I trust totally. My mom is safe. God is with her. How could I have made it without Lissa? She is a vital force, a calming, comforting force. The power of touch is extraordinary and so simple. Sean continues to climb. The birds continue to sing.

Back inside, we take a seat opposite the surgery doors. My mom will be out soon. Dr. Strasen walks out into the hallway and spots us. As she moves in our direction, I wonder what the news is going to be. I study her face. She crouches on the floor directly in front of me and looks up into my eyes. Without hesitation, she speaks the words I do not want to hear.

"It was necessary for me to take the breast."

I close down. The doctor continues.

"There was additional lymph node involvement..."

She has lost me. I have taken in "cancer" and "we had to remove her breast." This is all I can handle. Tears well. I ask if I can see her now.

"Let me go see," the doctor says softly. Moments later, she re-appears and signals for me to come in.

"Can I come, too?" Sean begs. Dr. Strasen shakes her head gently, "Not right now. You'll be able to see her soon though." With the metal doors closing behind us, I am wrenched by his plea, "Please?"

I walk swiftly toward her gurney and pull back on the curtain. There she is, eyes wide open.

"Hi Mom! How are you doing?" I'm ecstatic and begin to cry. Then I realize what a stupid question to ask but I have to hear her voice.

"I'm fine. Did you call everyone on the list yet?"

"No, no, not yet. But I will, Mom. You okay?"

"Yeah."

I want to know if she knows that it was cancer, but I am unable to ask. I grope for words.

"Sean cannot wait to see you."

"I want to see him, too!"

We are quiet a moment. My head spins. Has the doctor told her? If so, does she understand?

"Janet, can you make the calls now?"

"Yes, I'll go make the calls."

"Thank you," she says with a flick of her wrist, gesturing me out of the room.

As I leave the recovery room, she says, "Tell everyone I said hello."

I can't believe this, but suspect some residual anesthesia. She is so cute. She looks like a living angel.

I use Lissa's cell phone and am grateful not to call from a pay phone attached to the wall in a hallway of the hospital. The hardest calls are to my father and his wife, and my siblings. There is nothing like the confirmation that comes from speaking the words, "Cancer. They had to remove her breast." I cry after each call.

"Grammy!"

I turn to see Sean running toward the gurney being wheeled out of recovery. He grabs the railing and walks with them to her room. After a brief visit, we leave and let her sleep. It has been a long day for all. Sean and I climb into the van. He immediately drops into a deep, deep sleep.

Back in Cambria, I reflect on Lissa's wise words. "Remember, Janet, the cancer is your mom's thing. Don't take it on." She's right.

Returning to the hospital at sunset, the world holds a mystical quality that gives me the gift of peace. The setting sun has magically painted the mountains, the sky, and the sea. I drive in awe of their beauty. Parked off to the side of the road, I notice lovers and wish I were one of them.

Entering the hospital, tired but grateful, I walk down the same corridor, this time completely relaxed. Strolling into her room, I see my mom as she faces her dinner tray. On it is a whole chicken breast. I cut it for her, and am saddened to realize she can't use her right arm at all. Despite my warning for her to slow down, she devours the chicken, vegetables, a dinner roll, a huge brownie, and a cup of coffee. She eats as if nothing has happened.

"Janet, grab a paper and pen. I have a few questions for the doctor. First question: What happens now after cancer has been confirmed by pathology? In the same breath, she says to me, "I turned on Oprah. It was about over-achiever kids and their parents."

I smile. She continues dictating. I finish her list of questions. Mom agrees I should go on home. I am coming down fast, and I know it. I kiss her cheek, tell her I love her, and am out the door, grateful that she will be coming home tomorrow.

~ 15 ~

THE DAYS FOLLOWING

May 26, 2001

A Note from Janet's Journal:

Woke up at 8:30 a.m. and called the hospital. Mom was awake and ready to come home. In fact, she had been up since 4:00 that morning, walking the halls. While I was on the phone with her, she said,

"Oh, just a minute. Sir. Excuse me! I had a full breakfast this morning, but it wasn't enough. I'd like an egg salad sandwich."

"Yes, okay," hearing the man in the background respond.

"You amaze me, Mom! I'll be there for you soon."

"Okay, I'll be ready."

Hanging up, I began to clean the kitchen. The phone rings off the hook. Worried friends and relatives. I ended up leaving thirty minutes late and then got lost in the woods trying to find Kayla's house where I was dropping Sean off for the morning.

The drive to the hospital was as beautiful as the day before, but without the added stress. I remembered driving closely behind Lissa's car. I remembered seeing the silhouette of my mom's small head in the rear window. I shook the events of yesterday from my mind.

Walking into the hospital, I was again flooded with the memories of yesterday. I made my way into her room. Her bed sat unmade and empty. A rush of adrenalin.

Oh, my God, what happened to her? My immediate thoughts were that she had died and no one could contact me. Suddenly, something off to my left catches my eye. She sat in a chair, glowing and radiant like never before. Angelic.

"I've been ready for an hour!" She smiles.

"Oh, I am so sorry, Mom."

"It's okay. I've made several Reiki contacts."

Still shaking, I notice a nurse approaching. She asks my mom if she wanted a wheelchair. I couldn't wait for this one!

Grabbing her overnight bag, I tell her I will go and get the car.

Turning back down the long corridor I picked up my pace. Thrilled, I wanted to skip, even run. Sensing someone on my tail, I turned around. My mom was on my heels. I couldn't believe it. In my excitement, I asked, "How do you feel, Mom?"

"Very blessed. I may have lost a breast but I gained my soul."

Struck by her words, I paused briefly in contemplation as we left the hospital.

We had a nice drive home through the enchanted forest, the vineyards, and the rolling hills leading to Highway 1. How good it felt to have her in the car! Being in the moment. Enjoying life as it unfurled. A new beginning.

The rest of the day was quiet. Sean remained at Kayla's. Mom and I ate and slept. I loved hearing her snore from her bedroom upstairs. I felt comforted.

May 27, 2001
A Letter from Vee's Journal:
Dear God,

Thank You, God, for being with me in the hospital. What a feeling of peace. Abundant joy following. So many friends joining us in the unfold-ment. The right people are in my life at the present showing their love and concern. I could feel a band of angels surrounding me and feeding my spirit throughout my sojourn in the hospital and beyond.

As Margaret Butterworth said on my answering machine, "You have it all behind you now." A good point!

My Zen Bear from my friend, Lissa, sits beside me in contemplation of the mysteries of life. There are many.

This morning I shall go for a walk among my favorite trees, or perhaps on the ranch with the wild flowers popping up everywhere.

Thank You for my family. They are so precious and supportive.

Thank You for my abundant health.

My Sincere Self.

May 27, 2001

A Note from Janet's Journal:

I am back at home and the sun is setting. I feel exhausted and relieved, beaten and invigorated. Sitting down in my orange chair, I find it hard to believe that I had picked my mom up from the hospital just yesterday. Jessa is with her now. I left after buying her groceries and things. Jessa rented a movie, cleaned out her fireplace, and built her a nice fire. I was happy to have given her the rest of my woodpile, which Jessa neatly stacked.

I am grateful for all the people in Cambria who prayed for her, who brought her food, flowers, and cards, or came by simply to do the dishes.

A Letter from Janet's Journal, *same time*:

Dear Mom,

I just want you to know how good it felt to do things for you. Washing your hair today was wonderful. Massaging your scalp and rinsing your hair. I loved every minute of it. Shopping for you and washing your dishes. I am sure Jessa feels just as good doing all those things for you, too.

I love you and am glad you are home. Sleep tight, snore away, and dream pleasant dreams. I will plan to visit you in a couple of weeks to see how you are doing.

Until next time.

Love you, Me

An Afternoon in July 2001 ~ Janet

Now, months since my mother's surgery, I find myself climbing up into my son's tree fort. Leaning back, I lay my bare feet against the massive trunk, once again asking for guidance. Am I ready to take the next step? Maybe. Am I as frail as I was back on January 3, 2000? No. Can I ask for courage and strength? Yes. Will it be scary? Perhaps. Can I take the next step without my mom? Yes. Am I alone? Absolutely not. Will I fall? Maybe.

There comes a time in a woman's life where she must go off on her own. She must release her mother in order to do this. In parting, one does not lose the other. If anything, appreciation is born, the love deepens. Gazing up into this giant old oak, I see the strongest branches splay off in two directions. They do not become separate. They are joined and rooted, and the roots are deep. The time has come now for my mother and I to branch out, to reach for our own piece of the sky, always knowing we will never lose our connection. I've come a long way in my journey.

The tears that bathe me are joyous. Reflecting back just three days ago, I captured it all. My memory jumps to that moment I was pulling away from my mother's home. She was in a different place this time. So was I. Standing on the slope of forest just behind her home, she leaned forward, hands on her knees, childlike, yelling, "I love YOU more than you love me!" As always, Sean yelled back from the passenger window, "I love YOU more than you love me!" For the first time, I joined in. And as I tooted the car horn and looked back at her, I didn't sob thinking this would be the last time I would ever see her. This time, I smiled. There she stood radiating God's love and light. She was illuminated, animated, playful, joyous. Pure love danced there in that woodland. This image will never leave me, nor will my life ever be the same.

My heart tells me it is time. Letting go, I am willing to take the next step.

In the stillness, the wind churns its way powerfully through the leaves of this magnificent oak. God's orchestra. A commanding applause!

EPILOGUE

Janet

As I embark on the final pages of this book, I delight in the myriad of gifts that have transpired over the years since that call back on January 3, 2000. If God had shown up that day and said, "Well, Janet, are you ready for the big one?" Without hesitation I would have adamantly replied, "Not today, but maybe another time." And then, I would have run like hell. But the truth is this. God did make an appearance on that day and yes, there was a confrontation, an internal war that as I've said earlier, at some point necessitated surrender.

On my journey to acceptance, surrendering became a process and there was nothing speedy about it. In all honesty, I believe it took a long time because of my resistance. Over the years, I floated along in the currents of fear and doubt and then suddenly found myself in the abyss of the deepest ocean in the world. Rapids and tumultuous undercurrents ripped my whole world apart. It was there in the darkness that I would face the most profound fears of my life. I witnessed the chaotic nature of my mind as it held on to that which I had absolutely no control over, nor answers for. Would my mom live through this or would she die? Would I lose complete control of my emotions? Could I survive without her in my world?

At times while surfacing there would be no shore in sight, while at other times I would reach the shore weathered from the storm, only to be yanked back down to the depths. But it was also there in the dark that I would find the stillness, and in the stillness I connected with Spirit.

In my efforts to understand, to grasp what could possibly be in it that would offer me a life lesson seemed futile. Much less a gift. Today, I rejoice and give thanks for the many gifts that are still being bestowed upon me since this episode in my life. Alchemy occurred and with it brought many unexpected miracles. If this is what it took to become who I am today, I have no regrets.

I truly believe the events in our lives all happen as synchronous moments. Each and every one. And through these events, life becomes an increasingly worthwhile experience. My journey has indeed become sacred.

I'm glad I didn't run!

EPILOGUE

Vee

I began my soul's journey into wellness decades ago.
Four and a half years ago, I discovered the mass in
my breast and needed to reach even more deeply into
my spiritual core to find healing. I felt a force
directing me. A deep yearning to know and

experience my truth formed the foundation of my search.

On this quiet Sunday afternoon, a feeling of tranquility floods my being. Sitting in the garden I share with the squirrels and blue jays, I take in the miracle of nature. The ivy-covered arbor covering the path to my doorway embraces the deer as well as friends, family, and clients. Beside the front door, the red Begonia tumbles out of its window box, an array of bold color more beautiful than ever. I marvel at the grand design of creation. Sipping my tea, I reflect upon my own Divine blueprint for life.

We are born and we die—all of us. And between those points, we live our lives and grow our souls. A favorite Chinese proverb reads, "Our destiny, or allotted time, is sealed; and when the door closes on life, it is by mandate of heaven." In my allotted time, I have journeyed far. Now, and until my door closes, I am blessed to live in joy and peace.

Today, here in my garden, I own a deeper understanding of the process that led me from one choice to another as I savor each precious moment of life.

Although my life continues to embrace a physical challenge, it is filled with a world of sacred places. I still dream dreams and have visions of beauty and wonder.

We always have choice. I have chosen to go within when faced with a decision, being the only one who can know the needs of my soul. Here is a verbal hug to my family and friends for allowing me to do this. The inner truth reveals only love.

I have chipped and pecked away at the shell of my limitation, and in the shattering of the pieces; a new, more enlightened self broke free.

A red setting hen in her diligence was an awesome teacher!

The End

"Every mother contains her daughter in herself
and every daughter her mother, and every
woman extends backward into her mother
and forward into her daughter."

            __Carl Jung

The Green Velvet Journals

Our parallel journeys are simultaneously separate and intertwined. They reveal emotional truth, the frailty of life itself, and the joining and parting of two women with an extraordinary bond.

The journeys have been sad and joyous, difficult and wondrous, debilitating and empowering, defeating and transcendent. All of this takes time, it takes work, and it takes love.

"For all those dancing with breast cancer, I wish you purity of heart and clear vision. May the stars shine down upon you as they do for me. " **Vee**

In loving gratitude, I acknowledge the following people….

My father, John D. Riley, for his enthusiasm and encouragement throughout this project of love and determination.

My father's wife, and my dear friend, Janice Miller, for all her encouragement, love, and support.

My twin sister, Karen Riley, for all those times she listened while I rambled on in fear a thousand miles away.

My sister, Jessa Riley, for her unbelievable courage to be the woman she was meant to be.

My Beloved son, Sean Mauk, who sheds love and light wherever he goes. His smile, while delivering the "rejection letters" from the mailbox, kept me going. I will love him always.

My Mom. I think it's time for some chocolate!

The many wonderful souls who were in my life during the time of struggle and acceptance.

The journey continues…

"Kate" aka Janet
December 2003

Heartfelt thanks to the following people...

My Reiki friends, Jan Alexander, Nan Ferreira, Jane Wheeler, and Judith Brandt. Restoration in mind, body, and spirit, occurred on many occasions with their healing touches.

Lissa McConnell, so gentle in her loving-kindness for all Beings. A true friend.

The spirit-filled souls at Unity Church in Cambria, whose love and prayers continue to sustain me. The late Margaret Butterworth. Memory of her abides with me to this day.

My surgeon, Dr. Michelle Strasen, for giving medical suggestions while allowing me to follow my heart.

My children: Janet, for the green velvet journal, a gift of grace that held within its pages the depths of my soul; Jessa and Karen, for their quiet and loving support.

My angels and guides who have been close-by on this amazing journey.   **Vee**

December 2003

The Green Velvet Journals

ABOUT THE AUTHORS

Author Vee Riley is a Reiki master/teacher, massage therapist, artist, and writer currently making plans to relocate to Sun Valley, Idaho, where she plans to continue her healing work . In her new home, nestled in the mountains, she will teach Reiki and massage, as well as leading retreats in the field of healing, story-telling, and the mother/daughter journey.

Author Kate Riley realized her passion for writing while attending Antioch University Santa Barbara, California. She has recently returned to her place of birth, Boise, Idaho, and is currently leading women's writing groups while working on her first novel.

Both Vee and Kate are available for ongoing workshops, signings, and speaking engagements.

In The Beam Publishing House
P. O. Box 2313
Boise, ID. 83701

The Green Velvet Journals

Give the gift of

The Green Velvet Journals

Purchase your copy of *The Green Velvet Journals*. Order by credit card at www.thegreenvelvetjournals.com.

Name _____

Address _____

City _____

State _____ Zip _____

Phone (___) _____

Quantity	Price	Subtotal
#_____ @ $16.95 each:		$ _____
Idaho residents, add sales tax:		$ _____ (6%)
Shipping & Handling:		$ _____ 3.50
($1.95/per additional book)		$ _____
Total Enclosed:		$ _____

Please make your check payable to Vee Riley or Kate Riley and return to:

In The Beam Publishing House
c/o Riley & Riley
P. O. Box 2313
Boise, ID. 83701

Printed in the United States
16501LVS00003B/55-132

9 780974 914107